RETALIATION

AMY BLOCK JOY

ISBN: 1482651335
ISBN 13: 9781482651331
Library of Congress Control Number: 2013904440
CreateSpace Independent Publishing Platform
North Charleston, South Carolina
Printed by CreateSpace

"Each time I find myself flat on my face, I pick myself up and get back in the race …"

—That's Life
Song written by Dean Kay and Kelly Gordon, 1964
Sung by Frank Sinatra, 1966

Contents

Author's Note

Retaliation is my personal account of activities that took place after I blew the whistle on fraud in my workplace. The events and conversations reported are based on my own recollections as well as published articles and reports and documents that I have reviewed. Names and identifying information for some people and entities involved have been changed. In quoted materials, these substitutions appear in [brackets].

This book presents my personal view on whistleblower retaliation. I wrote this book to educate others on a significant and common consequence of reporting wrongdoing. Although this book takes place in an institution of higher learning, retaliation can happen to anyone, in any position, and in any organization.

When I blew the whistle, I thought I prepared myself for the onslaught. However, I could not have imagined the nature, the magnitude, or ferociousness of what took place.

Fraud continues to be an institutional threat. Reporting wrongdoing is just too dangerous, and many well-meaning employees decide to look the other way. Effective safeguards are needed to prevent retaliation from becoming the reason for silence.

I'm hoping this book will provide understanding that retaliation is a serious threat to employees as well as to institutional reputation and credibility. Even with laws, regulations, and anti-retaliation policies in place, employees fear the retribution that comes with speaking out.

And lastly, I want to encourage anyone venturing down this dark path not to give up. Change takes time. Find someone you trust and tell your story.

Acknowledgments

First and foremost, I want to thank my daughter who continues to be the shining light in my life. Her incredible strength of character, integrity, generosity, and dedication to helping those in need have kept me focused on the things that truly matter.

Second, to my developmental editor, Alan Rinzler, who guided me in the telling of this difficult story. I am forever grateful for his clear and inspiring direction in helping me to find my voice.

And much gratitude to Eric Rayman, Esq., my literary attorney. Thank you for your insight and wisdom.

I also want to acknowledge my many friends who continue to support me. Thank you Daniel Ellsberg for your courage to speak out about the truth. And to David Cole and Mary Lee Cole, at Bay Tree Publishing, I appreciate all you have done to support my *Whistleblower* book.

In addition, I appreciate the special care provided by my copy editor, Leslie Tilley.

And lastly, to the all the investigators and officials from the provost's office, I want to thank you for protecting my rights as a university employee and for listening. I'm hoping that with the new leadership at UC Davis, more will be done to educate the campus community on ways to prevent and stop retaliation.

Prologue: Whistleblower

In August 2006, I became a whistleblower. That decision was easy: it was the right thing to do. But, as it turns out, being a whistleblower isn't a great career move.

As a faculty member at the University of California, Davis, and a twenty-eight–year employee, I thought the university would thank me. I was surprised that the investigation took four years and that during most of that time I was fighting to keep my job.

For a decade before blowing the whistle, I was happily directing a statewide program for low-income families called the Food Stamp Education Program. My multimillion-dollar nutrition program assisted families up and down the state of California. I believed that my work was making a difference in the lives of many people.

Then, suddenly everything changed. The moment I exposed the criminal activity, I became the enemy.

Initially, I tried to report the wrongdoing internally, but I was silenced by my boss, the department chair. So I filed a whistleblower report. My four-page report unleashed a firestorm of resistance and collusion culminating in retaliation and retribution.

During the criminal investigation, I discovered that alerting the university to whistleblower retaliation activities didn't make it stop. The people involved in the retaliation believed their behavior was justified and no one stepped in to tell them otherwise.

Over the long haul, I worried that the retaliation might be an indicator of something much more sinister. Were the retaliators trying to conceal something? Who was involved? Had I unearthed some sort of corruption?

This book is my personal story about retaliation. But first some background on the whistleblowing case that led up to it.

February 2006

In the early afternoon of February 27, 2006, I was working in my office on the UC Davis campus. At age 53, I was proud of my UC Berkeley undergrad and graduate education. I'd also climbed the ladder of success as director of a $14 million dollar statewide program.

I dug into my briefcase looking for a proposal that I'd been working on at home. Having left the four-page document at home, sixty miles away, I called Beverly Benford, my trusted administrative coordinator and budget manager, to get a copy from our office files.

"Beverly, could you bring me a copy of my impact study proposal from last year?"

"Right away," Beverly replied without a pause. And about five minutes later she knocked on my door and handed me a copy. We'd been working side by side for the past twelve years and she had always been very responsive and loyal.

"Working at home again!" she said winking at me. She was aware that my job was a continuous treadmill of activity. There were always deadlines and surprises along the way.

"Never a dull moment," I answered, smiling in response. I was fond of Beverly and loved the energy that she created.

"Aren't you taking a lunch break?" she asked, looking concerned. Like a mother hen, she was always telling me that I was way too thin.

We both heard her telephone ringing in her office just then, and she left in a hurry to answer it.

Her office, located next door to my private office suite, was part of a large room where all the program files were stored. About twenty large file cabinets were filled with the last seven years' of program records required by our funding agency, the United States Department of Agriculture (USDA). Beverly watched over those files like a hawk.

I heard her answer the phone and then make some directive to her staff. Beverly's three staff members were housed in small desks right next to the files. Ginny Buckner was Beverly's program assistant, Ryan Holt was her IT guy, and Rebecca Fukumoto was her budget superstar. These dedicated professionals were kept by Beverly on a very tight leash.

I turned my attention to look at the file copy and observed almost immediately that it was different than the one I'd left at home. On page 2, a handwritten note in the margin of the budget spreadsheet stuck out like a sore thumb. The amount of $150,000 in Beverly's own handwriting was next to her notation "For RS." RS, or Raymond Savage, was my supervisor and the department chair.

I also noted that at the bottom of that spreadsheet my $60,000 total budget had been increased to $210,000. Yikes! A difference of exactly $150,000. What a coincidence. That can't be right!

Alarmed, I sprinted up two flights of stairs to talk to my boss, Dr. Raymond Savage, chair of the Food, Health, and Society Department. His door was open and I walked right in. Raymond looked up. Blond and stocky, he was wearing one of his Hawaiian shirts with large pink flowers.

I handed him the spreadsheet with Beverly's handwritten notation. He took it and gave it a glance.

"Do you see the notation in the margin?" I asked.

"It's a math error," he said and waved it off not even looking at me. "Have Beverly fix it," he said, handing it back while standing up. This was a signal for me to leave.

At the time, I had a rock solid conviction that Raymond, a top-notch scientist and savvy administrator, could do no wrong. It would have been difficult for me to believe otherwise as I was from the old school of "don't rock the boat."

I went back down the stairs and showed the spreadsheet to Beverly. She blamed Rebecca for the error and said it would be fixed immediately. Although there was no reason for me not to believe her, I decided to document the mistake and its correction in a letter, which I emailed to Raymond that same day.

He replied to my email: "Your letter is fine."

A gnawing concern kept me at work until Beverly left the office that afternoon. I wanted to inspect the office files. After I heard Beverly's footsteps leaving her office, I went into the file room. All the drawers were locked and I didn't have a key.

The next morning, I asked Beverly for the key. After she unlocked the files, I sat down in the file room and opened a drawer. It didn't take more than five minutes to pick out a file with Raymond Savage's name on it. In the file, I discovered a purchase order that knocked my socks off! Hiding my discovery in my purse, I went back to my private office to make a telephone call.

I called Fry's Electronics. At the time, I was surprised that we used this local electronics store as a university vendor.

"What's a Canon Optura?" I asked Dave, the Fry's employee who answered the telephone. Beverly had written "Canon Optura" as the product description. The price: $1400! Dave told me that the item was a DVD camcorder. This piece of video-making equipment wasn't an allowable program purchase.

Beverly had purchased a very expensive item. The PO, dated November 2005, had other red flags. My approval wasn't on the PO, and it lacked a clear description of the item. Beverly had approved the purchase and certified her own approval—and again, in her own handwriting, she'd noted "pick up"! This purchase would be considered personal.

March 2006

I couldn't sleep for the next two days. I was concerned that Beverly had committed some kind of embezzlement, allocating special funds to herself on the pretense of buying equipment for office use. Much as I didn't want to contemplate what my conscience was screaming, I couldn't imagine another reasonable explanation.

After more soul searching, I decided I had to act fast and find out what was really going on.

I arranged a routine meeting with Beverly and Raymond for March 2. Before the meeting, I'd prepared a short letter to confront Beverly on her unapproved purchase. I wanted for her to explain this purchase in front of the department chair. At 3 p.m., in Raymond's office, I handed Beverly and Raymond a copy of the PO and my letter.

"As director, I feel I must provide a written record of a concern that I'm bringing to your attention." I read the letter out loud.

"Here are the facts ... On November 18, 2005, an item was purchased that appears ... for personal use ... not a legitimate business expense."

My letter alleged that Beverly had made an unapproved personal purchase for a $1400 DVD camcorder, which I considered to be a misuse of federal funds. In addition, she'd violated university policy when she improperly approved and certified her own purchase.

After I read the letter, I turned to Beverly, took a deep breath, looked her in the eye, and asked, "Where is the DVD camcorder?"

She answered, "It's in my garage."

As I'd read, Raymond appeared initially stunned and held his head down. He emerged from his stupor after Beverly left the room. At that point, he staunchly defended her.

"This is no big deal. I've been through this with many employees. This isn't anything world-shattering," he said.

He called it poor judgment and suggested that I was trying to get Beverly in trouble. I found his response confusing. He seemed to be angry at me! I insisted that we change Beverly's responsibilities, and he reluctantly agreed.

"You owe it to your friendship with Beverly and to the program to try to find a way to forgive her," he told me. He was confident that she'd buckle down to business and regain my trust.

The next day Beverly accepted responsibility for the misuse, wrote a letter of apology, said that this was a one-time transgression, and made out a check to the UC Regents.

April 2006

In April, my discomfort increased when Beverly begged me not to cash the check she had given me as reimbursement for her embezzlement, as she didn't have enough funds in her account. When he heard about this, Raymond suggested that he pay for the DVD camcorder and then Beverly could pay him back when she had the money.

Neither Beverly nor Raymond appeared to be taking the issue seriously, so I went back to the files and dug deeper. I found another incident of misuse by Beverly. She'd purchased a stereo system in March 2005. Again this wasn't on our list of approved equipment and had the exact same red flags. I wrote a warning letter to Beverly to document the second misuse of funds and met with Raymond. After he refused to report it upward, as required by policy, we argued.

"This happened a long time ago, March 2005," Raymond angrily snapped. "This one doesn't count!"

"Raymond," I said unmoved by his desire to give Beverly another chance, "it doesn't matter *when* this happened. It's called stealing!"

After receiving my warning letter, a tearful and remorseful Beverly took full responsibility for the misuse of funds. She begged for my forgiveness and put all of this in writing.

Beverly's work improved and she appeared contrite and remorseful. I, however, suffered. A great cloud of unease disturbed my ability to concentrate on my work. Distressed, I sent an email to Raymond requesting permission to report the misuse upward in the university's hierarchy to the college dean's office. I told him that I felt my integrity was being compromised. I believed he'd either grant my request or report it himself.

It never occurred to me that there was a third option.

May 2006

Chair Raymond Savage, still protecting Beverly, sent me to consult with his ally and colleague, the vice-chair, Dr. Fred Stone. I met with Fred on May 8th. Fred, a jovial, heavyset older professor was a graduate of the school of hard knocks.

Fred got it immediately. Finally someone was going to do something!

"Write a third warning letter to Beverly and put in the letter the definition of *embezzlement*," he told me, hinting that he was going to terminate her himself. He promised to report the issue to the dean's office.

"Two purchases in 2005 are bad enough," he said, adding, "She has to go."

However, like Raymond, in the end, he made excuses and stonewalled my attempts to get the wrongdoing exposed.

June 2006

In June, after Fred told me that Beverly was crying to other faculty that I'd accused her of stealing, I insisted that her check be cashed. Beverly managed to find funds to pay back the university. I took her March 2006 check made out to the UC Regents to the cashier's office on campus. Our departmental accountant certified my explanation: personal check from employee Beverly Benford to pay back the university for personal equipment purchases.

July 2006

Beverly went on vacation in July, just after recruiting for a new staff member. Terence, a young manager, was to join our staff later in August. I was also out of the office having surgery for skin cancer. While I was working at home, Beverly returned from vacation and, according to Fred, was spreading rumors about my health.

August 2006

In mid-August, I received a phone call that Beverly was back to purchasing equipment! I returned to Davis on August 24 to strip Beverly of all her responsibilities. I gave Beverly another letter. That evening, Ginny Buckner, one of her staff, called me at home.

"I need to tell you something," she said whispering over the telephone. "I now report to you, not Beverly. You are my boss, right?" she asked after a short pause.

"Yes," I answered intrigued.

"Well," I heard her gulp. "Are you sitting down?"

"Beverly's been getting travel reimbursements for trips she never took," she told me adding, "She'd fire me if she knew I told you."

"What!"

"It's true," she said, and hung up.

Shocked by the very idea that Beverly could be turning in phony travel vouchers for reimbursement, I drove to Davis at sunrise the next morning to conduct an audit at the university's accounts payable office. Beverly, an office administrator, sat at a desk all day long—she wasn't traveling!

After a review at the Davis accounting office where travel reimbursements were stored, I discovered that she'd been falsifying trips all over California. Outraged by the possibility that another $20,000 in travel fraud would tip the scales to high-level criminal behavior, I met with the newly appointed chair, Fred Stone, and demanded that he report the allegations immediately.

"Look at this one," I said pointing to the travel reimbursement for picking up a broken computer in Bakersfield. "She was reimbursed for $800 when we didn't even have a computer to be picked up in Bakersfield." I was beside myself with dismay.

"Didn't anyone question why we're paying an administrator who sits at a desk to drive three hundred miles and pick up a broken computer?"

Fred said that Raymond Savage had approved her travel reimbursements, adding quickly that Raymond also believed her travel looked suspicious.

Fred seemed unmoved by my plea to report the misuse of funds to the dean's office. He warned me to "do nothing" until I heard from him.

"This is my job," he said sternly, "not yours." Clearly, Fred wasn't going to report it even though the theft allegations had increased to over $20,000!

That night, morally outraged, I filed a whistleblower report with the UC Davis chancellor's office. I downloaded two forms: Exhibit A: Improper Activities Report—Whistleblower, and Exhibit B: Retaliation or Interference Complaint.

Exhibit A, a one-page form with space for name, home address, home telephone, payroll title, supervisor's name, had two inches of space to report the "alleged improper activity that is requested for review."

I completed the form and wrote in the space: "Embezzlement and Travel Fraud: see attached report" and attached my three-page Whistleblower Report and documentation: DVD camcorder purchase order signed by Beverly, my letter to Beverly and Raymond reporting the embezzlement on March 2nd, Beverly's letter of apology, photocopy of her check to the UC Regents, stereo purchase order signed by Beverly, and copies of four falsified travel reimbursement forms that were signed by Beverly and Dr. Raymond Savage. In my report I estimated the total amount of fraud to be $22,000 (two issues of embezzlement for $2000 and travel fraud estimated to be $20,000). I signed and dated Exhibit A.

Exhibit B was also a one-page form for protection against retaliation and included this statement: 'I swear under penalty of perjury that the contents of this complaint are true to the best of my knowledge.' I signed and dated the form. Having read about whistleblowers on the Internet, I knew to expect retaliation as part of the job!

In addition to filing the form with the chancellor's office, I mailed copies to Raymond Savage (former chair) and Fred Stone. I also sent copies to the executives at the dean's office: Dr. Percy Grossman (associate dean of the college), Shirley Handover (director of human resources), Dr. Lorenzo Maestro (visiting academic dean from the University of Rome, Italy), and Dr. Gabriel Fitzpatrick (dean of the college).

The next day, Saturday, August 26, Fred called me at home in the late afternoon to tell me that he and Raymond were going to meet with Beverly on Wednesday.

"It's too late," I interrupted. "I've sent a whistleblower report."

"What?" I heard Fred breathing rapidly on the telephone. "What did you send?"

"Everything," I replied in one word. "I've sent the chancellor everything!"

The next day, Fred, going on the defense, distributed a long email to various high-level officials in the dean's office explaining that he and Raymond had been suspicious of Beverly's travel and that she'd continued to engage in embezzlement activities. He requested that the investigation not interrupt the important research in his department.

Relieved that the alleged crimes would now be investigated, I arrived at work on Monday expecting that the dean's office would take care of the leave-notification process. My relief was short lived: they failed to assist and left me in the lurch. I didn't feel it was in the best interest of the university for me to interact with Beverly on such an inflammatory issue. I also worried that important evidence could be destroyed. The situation was fraught with conflict.

On August 28, after several failed attempts to get the attention of the dean's office, I rounded up two witnesses in the department, April Jefferson and Jerry Fields, to provide assistance. I went to Beverly's office and in the presence of April and Jerry, gave her a letter that said she was on paid investigatory leave for two weeks.

"This letter confirms that you are being placed on paid investigatory leave effective today, August 28, 2006. You are hereby relieved of all work duties ... for two to three weeks."

After a lot of hemming and hawing and repeatedly demanding to talk to "Ray," as she now called him, Beverly was finally persuaded that she really did need to pack up and go home. She wasn't upset in the slightest. Clearly she must have been tipped off about what was going to happen.

Beverly even tried to contact Ray using her university-issued BlackBerry just before turning it over to me. As I took the BlackBerry from her, she flashed an angry look at me and said, "You just wait …" I saw the name Savage on the screen and turned it off.

During the hourlong leave process, Beverly tried to remove some files from one of her locked desk drawers to take home. After arguing with her about what she could and couldn't take, I managed to take the files out of her box. I opened a red file folder. The first page in the file was covered in my name! She'd been practicing my signature. Her forgery was shockingly authentic looking!

Jerry carried a box of Beverly's personal belongings to her car while April, the other witness, took the files Beverly had tried to take home directly to the dean's office. Shirley Handover, the director of Human Resources, who was now the official in charge, was very tight-lipped. When I met with her later, she wouldn't give me a copy of Beverly's forgery.

I returned to the department and went upstairs to let Fred know that Beverly was on investigatory leave. Raymond was out of town.

"Beverly is enraged at you," he reported, and he didn't look so happy himself.

"You spoke to her?" I said without thinking.

"You can't tell me what to do," he began, then added, "Raymond and I will be meeting with her on Wednesday."

I decided not to engage any further in conversation with Fred about the investigation.

I went downstairs to my office, eager to return to the work that I'd dedicated my career to—helping low-income families by securing another year of funding for the program.

I tried to get the dean's office to secure the evidence, but no one responded to my request. Since I was put in charge of the notification, I secured the evidence in Beverly's office by sealing her desk drawers and cabinets with duct tape. I also put everything from my office that I thought might be evidence into the trunk of my car. Before I drove home late that night, I even put a strip of scotch tape across the gap between my office door and the top of the frame.

The next morning I found the tape on my office door broken and my boxes and files scattered all over the office. I sent an email to the HR director that my office had been ransacked. She never replied.

September 2006

On September 3, 2006, Labor Day, I was called at home by one of the deans from the college. Dean Percy Grossman came over to my house and in the driveway served me with a letter. After removing the letter from the dean's office's tobacco-colored envelope, Dean Grossman instructed me to read it out loud. The vaguely worded letter informed me that a whistleblower had alleged that I'd engaged in improper government activities at UC Davis.

> September 1, 2006
>
> Dear Dr. Joy:
>
> I have been informed that a whistleblower report has been filed alleging you engaged in improper business activities at UC Davis ... I am directing you to refrain from performing your administrative and management responsibilities ...

I was warned not to speak to anyone, as I could be accused of interfering with a federal investigation. Fred Stone was put in charge of my program!

Fred told me later that after Beverly was put on investigatory leave she drove over to the auditor's office on campus and announced a crime! Unbeknownst to me, after Beverly left our office she went directly to Internal Auditing and filed a verbal whistleblower report against me!

This was the first of what I considered to be retaliatory activities taken against me. Unfortunately, there are no apparent safeguards protecting a whistleblower from false allegations, even from the very person under investigation. I was unprepared for the dramatic turn that took place the minute I filed my whistleblower report.

Two days after my visit from Dean Grossman, I met with the university auditors and turned over my evidence, including three letters, a copy of Beverly's check, two purchase orders, Beverly's two emails taking "full responsibility," copies of Beverly's alleged travel fraud, and my evidence documenting that Beverly's travel was fraudulent, since she was in her Davis office at the time she claimed she was traveling.

After my two-hour discussion of my evidence, the auditors reported the verbal whistleblower allegations made against me. Surprisingly, they were same allegations that I filed against Beverly. It would be easy to provide documentation to support my defense, as nothing that she alleged was true. It was Fred who affectionately named it "Beverly's Anti-Whistleblower Report."

At the end of the meeting, I was given permission to contact the USDA and let them know that some issues were being reviewed by Internal Auditing. I breathed a sigh of relief, since I'd been worried that the USDA wouldn't be informed properly and that I could be accused of trying to cover up a potential misuse of funds.

On September 14, I met with the UC Davis police, at their request. I was asked many questions about Raymond. One of the questions concerned his response when

I confronted Beverly about the first embezzlement incident, the purchase of the DVD camcorder.

"He was stunned," I told the detective in charge of the interview.

"Why do you think he was stunned?"

At that very moment, I realized that Raymond had given himself away. "He was stunned because I'd found out!" I said answering the question. Suddenly I figured out that it was *Raymond* who was in big trouble!

Apparently, while Beverly was embezzling and getting reimbursed for fake travel, he was getting her to approve large purchases for his department, hence the $150,000 notation on the spreadsheet. Unlike Beverly's, these purchases, at least as far as I could tell, were for the department and not for personal gain. This could be considered misappropriation of federal funds, since the purchases weren't approved by me and weren't allowable by the funding agency.

I was dumbfounded that this all happened behind my back. I would have never approved any of the fraudulent activities. Clearly, the deception and collusion allowed this criminal activity to go undetected for years.

October 2006

After I met many more times—with auditors, police, and federal agents—during October, a search warrant was served on Beverly on the early morning of October 30, a Monday. Federal agents seized $160,000 worth of stolen electronic goods at her residence. They also found evidence that she'd resold computers on the Internet. She resigned from her university job the next day, taking with her about $250,000 from her university pension.

I began to start to put the pieces of the program back together, with the help of my small team, Ginny, Rebecca, and Ryan. Terrence, the new hire, was out of the office, and I didn't expect that he'd have the stamina to stay the course.

November 2006

In early November I was officially cleared of all the allegations against me, which were unsubstantiated. No public announcement would be made, I was told, because of the confidential nature of the investigation. Unfortunately, many colleagues still held the mistaken perception that I'd been involved in the fraud.

Just before Thanksgiving the auditors conducted a surprise visit to the department and more fraud was uncovered. Fred continued to stop by my office to pass on gossip: Raymond's computer had been taken by the auditors. Dean Fitzpatrick had asked about the "missing money." And Beverly was still in contact with her faculty friends. I suspected that Fred's chit-chat was intended to provoke and upset me.

At this point, I believed more retaliatory activities were taken against me. I documented every one of them, hoping that the university would step in. My colleagues were avoiding me. Meetings were cancelled. Emails were ignored. My mailbox, usually brimming with letters and journals, was suddenly empty.

An attorney friend suggested that I seek legal counsel from an expert. The issues regarding whistleblower laws and the protection of whistleblowers from retaliation were complex, and I would require specialized advice.

I eventually found a terrific attorney named Michael A. Hirst, in Sacramento. He specialized in whistleblower cases and had previously worked as a Supervisory Assistant United States Attorney in California.

"My name is Amy Block Joy," I told Mr. Hirst in our first phone discussion that November, "and I've blown the whistle on fraud at the university."

I told him about the case, at least as much as I knew about at the time. "Because the fraud involved federal funds," I said, "it's being investigated by the U.S. Attorney's Office.

"The university has sent me letters telling me that I cannot talk to anyone," I confided. "They say I could be accused of interfering with a federal investigation," I whispered reading him the letter from September 1.

"I'm concerned that if the university knows that I've contacted an attorney, they won't talk to me," I added.

"If you prefer, we can work behind the scenes for as long as possible," Michael advised. "Send me the letter and a copy of your whistleblower report," he said.

"My first priority and goal is to keep my job and continue my work in helping vulnerable communities," I told Michael. "But it's really hard to do my job. No one will talk to me."

I hoped to work with the university channels as long as possible in order to get the matter resolved. I still had faith that the university would protect me.

That faith was largely the work of the university's locally designated official for whistleblowers, or LDO. Franklin Taylor-Starr, a vice-chancellor with official university clout, had been advising me on retaliation, and he was always prompt and courteous in his recommendations.

December 2006

In December, I took more evidence over to the auditor's office. Someone was putting documents into my mailbox anonymously.

In mid-December, I was asked by the auditors to review my emails. Apparently, Beverly had the password to my computer and been secretly using it beginning in 2001!

I asked Ryan if Beverly had been using my office when I was out of town.

"All the time," he answered. "She said she needed a private office, and while you were on sabbatical she became quite cozy in there."

I discovered in my sent box that Beverly had been forwarding hundreds of my emails to her computer. Beverly's ability to anticipate my every need wasn't based on her loyalty to me and the program. What she was actually doing was reading my email! This is when I began to see what I couldn't see before: I was conned big time!

January 2007

On January 1, 2007, my director position was moved to the dean's office. My new supervisor, Dean Percy Grossman, was a longtime ally and friend who knew me very well. I expected that this move would create a safe haven for my program. Working with Percy would be a godsend!

As I expected, Terrence didn't stay. Coincidentally, he resigned on my birthday.

February 2007

In February, a reporter from the *Sacramento Bee* left a voicemail message asking to interview me for a story on the Food Stamp Education Program. On February 20th, I was briefed by the university's legal team on what to say to the reporter regarding our program. The next day, I spoke for an hour with *Bee* reporter Carrie Peyton Dahlberg, and followed the university's advice to the letter, especially after she began to ask questions about Raymond Savage.

"Can you tell me about your budget?" Carrie interjected in the middle of a discussion about programmatic improvements in fruit and vegetable consumption.

"You'll have to talk to the university communications director," I said interrupting her. "Did I tell you about the evaluation results that showed our program was cost effective?" I added, making it clear that I wasn't going to be side tracked into talking about the investigation.

Carrie tried again: "How much funding is your department chair getting from the food stamp program?"

Shocked that she brought up my departmental chair, I scrambled for a reasonable answer.

"I really can't answer any budget questions. I suggest you talk to the university communications director," I said, this time providing the communications director's name and telephone number.

After the interview, I sent an email to the campus legal team letting them all know that someone had let the cat out of the bag. On February 23rd, the legal team sent an email to university employees about the media attention. The public exposure set off a frenzy of bizarre events:

> My car was vandalized in the university's parking lot. A forty-two-inch gash was carved along the passenger side of my Volvo.

> A negative letter about me was circulated up and down the state.

> A petition to remove me from office was widely distributed.

> Colleagues refused to work with me.

> Colleagues tried to deceive me by including me as an author on journal articles that I hadn't contributed to. I was alarmed when I accidentally found out. Were they trying to lay the groundwork to accuse me of scientific misconduct?

My research funding was terminated.

Account managers tried to intimidate me into illegally fixing departmental deficits.

I also received an unfriendly email from a colleague asking me to retrieve a three-hundred-pound laser printer from the hallway of the department. The auditors traced the purchase back to Beverly.

On the 23rd, I also received a tip from a friend that a petition to remove me from my director position was being faxed all over the state of California. I requested a copy of the document, and following approval from the university that I had a "need to know," Dean Grossman faxed it to my home on March 2.

Dated February 23, 2007, the four-page petition was signed by twenty-one of my colleagues. What alarmed me the most was that several of those who signed the petition had received and *spent* millions of dollars to assist low-income families under what they described as my "blatant mismanaged" leadership. This letter, in my mind, smacked of retaliation, but until an actual adverse action was taken against me by the university, I believed it was premature to consult with Mr. Hirst.

I was stunned by the accusations made by my former associates, who'd been my supporters *before* I blew the whistle. My personnel file and a hundred thousand emails documented that fact. Investigators poured through my employment history, personnel records, and emails looking for documentation of past complaints and other red flags. None were found.

My clean record showed twenty-two years of getting grants approved by federal funding agencies. Did my former associates and colleagues suddenly forget that I'd brought in and shared with them $120 million for work on hunger in California?

The friend who tipped me off to the petition told me that a couple of the signatories "wanted to take me down"—as though I was an elected politician to be humiliated and run out of town.

I called Percy, and he agreed that I could speak to one non-university person about retaliation. I wanted to consult with my neighbor, who happened to be the famous whistle-blower, Daniel Ellsberg. Daniel, who disclosed to the media (via "The Pentagon Papers") that the government had misled the public regarding the Vietnam War, warned me about re-taliation and how things could turn nasty and personal.

"Most likely you'll not regret what you did, but your life will be different," Daniel told me. "It's going to get harder. But don't despair when your friends desert you. All of it is unfortunate and irreversible. You'll be tested and re-tested and they'll try to break you," he continued.

"Few people will understand what you feel," he said. "But you'll sleep better at night knowing you did the right thing. Accept the new life and try to embrace it as an opportunity!"

Daniel gave me the courage to stand up for myself and fight for truth!

March 2007

On March 16, the *Sacramento Bee* published Carrie's news story on the front page. The article reported the fraud and an alleged cover-up by the department:

UCD worker accused of theft

A former UC Davis employee was indicted Thursday on one count of theft of govern-ment property, in a case that raises broader questions about how the university handled money for teaching the poorest Califor-nians. ... The woman, Beverly Benford, 65, of Sacramento, is suspected of a six-year spending spree of submitting fake travel expenses and buying consumer electronics. ... Benford told the *Bee* last week that she could not comment ... but in general all expenditures ... were approved by its director, [Amy] Block Joy. Yet it was Block Joy who filed a whistleblower complaint with the university, asking that the funding irregularities be investigated, according to a preliminary document which was given to the *Bee* by a law enforcement source in Yolo County. ... According to court documents the losses could total $160,000. ... In addition, UC Davis officials said they continue to investigate ... allegations that a campus department may have benefited improperly from large amounts of federal funds ... $798,826 ...

The AP news service spread the story up and down the state and across the nation, creating distress in many people associated with the university.

On March 15, a press release issued by the Justice Department reported Beverly Benford's indictment by a federal grand jury. She was being prosecuted by the U.S. Attorney Stephen Lapham, well known for his successful prosecution of the Unabomber. Through the Internet, I found out that she was released on bail pending a court hearing. We all wondered who had footed her $20,000 bond!

On March 21, Fred Stone sent round an email to the departmental faculty that he'd been asked to step down as of July 1. When Fred wrote "This was not my plan," everyone rushed in to defend him. From the barrage of emails sent to soothe poor ol' Fred, it was hard to miss that, once again, I was responsible.

The release of the news article generated enough angst that I spent the rest of March in isolation. Although still a member of the faculty in the Department of Food, Health, and Society, where the fraud took place, I was asked to keep away from departmental activities. All the people who'd been questioned about the fraud, my esteemed colleagues, were actively shunning me and appeared justified in doing so. Openly angry, they stonewalled my work-related requests to get back to business.

Percy's position regarding the petition was to wait and see. I met with Percy and Lorenzo Maestro, the visiting academic dean to discuss the letter. Percy indicated that he was going to speak to each of the signers. I provided names and telephone numbers of colleagues who'd indicated to me directly that they disagreed with the petition. I requested that they also be interviewed as well. Referring to the signatories as a "bunch of rambunctious folks," Percy told me not to worry about it.

But worry I did. I organized a conference call to get input from those who'd signed the petition. I wanted to hear what they had to say directly. Most of them didn't reply to my request. A couple had asked their staff members to take the call. As I waited for the conference group to gather, I put my telephone on speakerphone so one of my staff could take notes. That's when we heard a group whispering about "jumping ship." I didn't need a translator to understand that many believed my food stamp education program "ship" was sinking.

My plan to counter the proposed mutiny was to win everyone back by getting my program fully funded. I needed to get another year of support from the USDA. The decision about funds for 2008 would be made in September, and I still had a lot of work to do to renew the agency's trust. Having received a copy of a "damage control" email distributed nationally about the fraud, I *was* worried the program might fail. I felt responsible for the almost two hundred staff that worked in trenches and needed employment for themselves and their families. I knew that if my funding submerged, we'd all be in line for food stamps.

April 2007

On April 7, lame duck chair Fred Stone sent me a rambling email that was widely distributed. He accused me of various transgressions, some of them petty but many hinting of fraud. He also reported that Raymond was in big trouble for some sort of faculty misconduct allegation. I was taken aback by the email announcement. Even though Fred laid the blame for the allegations against Raymond on me, I wasn't the responsible party.

On April 12, after Fred's email went around, a meeting took place to discuss the fallout from his accusations. I was able to show Percy and visiting dean Maestro, from the dean's office, and others from the provost's office, that Fred's accusations were bogus. A few days later, the senior executive administrator (SEA) from the dean's office announced that the food stamp education program would be "reviewed." SEA Roland Babu was a highly respected accountant in the dean's office.

I'd been through this before: this was university-speak for "we need to have an administrative reason to get rid of you." Roland had been on the sidelines for the last six months, and I had no idea why he was suddenly in charge.

When I sent an email to Percy to ask him about the review, I received the strangest autoresponse: "Percy will be out for a while." He suddenly had gone to Botswana, leaving me to speculate if and when he'd return.

I did have confidence in Roland, having met him in 2006, after I blew the whistle. He had a solid reputation for being honest and was certainly the kind of authority figure that one holds in high esteem.

Like everyone else, Roland was uncomfortable with any mention of Beverly. It was impossible to avoid talking about her, since she'd created elaborate administrative systems to escape detection. During one meeting, I asked Roland if he'd ever met her. His response was very funny. "Nope, don't know her," he said wrinkling his nose with displeasure. "I wouldn't be able to pick her out of a lineup."

I decided that my best course of action would be to speak frankly to the review consultants. Since they weren't personally involved in the fraud, my hope was that they'd be able to find a fix for the program and let me get back to work.

On April 20, two consultants arrived in my office to interview me. They met with me first for an hour-and-a-half to talk about the needs of the program. For the next two hours, my team joined me in the room, and we engaged in a "group therapy" session. They appeared very sympathetic. Ginny, Ryan, Rebecca, and I told them exactly what happened. They looked as shocked as we felt. In the end, we felt grateful that someone cared enough to hear what we had to say.

I began to feel some level of optimism that we were on the verge of being rescued! My feeling seemed to be justified when the folks that had petitioned to remove me all requested large amounts of funding under my leadership.

I worked like a dog all spring. Although my colleagues were still rather stiff and cold, the thought of getting more money created enough of an incentive for them to respond to the budget request. I was eager to make good on my goal of having the program renewed by the USDA, and my small team, though exhausted, remained devoted to helping me reach this goal.

June 2007

We accomplished many positive activities in June. I conducted several trainings during that month with the help of my team. The sessions were very successful—at least that's what people wrote in their evaluations. I hoped that the tide had shifted and my critics were now back to business.

On June 26, Roland emailed me the organizational review of my food stamp education program. I was relieved to see attached to it an organizational chart that clearly had me at the top with my director title.

The report was very detailed and offered practical guidance for getting administrative pieces of the program in shape. I read it over several times and was thrilled that they recommended filling my staff vacancies.

Roland requested a meeting, and on June 27, I met with him and the HR director to go over the "organizational review," or, as I fondly called it, the OR. To me, the eight-page report appeared as sterile as a hospital operating room. The consultants mentioned the investigation but choose to ignore the chaos that resulted from my blowing the whistle.

One disturbing note was included: a comment from my colleagues about equipment being "lost" or "misplaced" by the state office under my leadership. It wasn't accurate. If the authors of the report, or even someone from the dean's office had been more forthcoming regarding the forty-page list of equipment that was "fraudulently purchased," I believe that comment might not have made it into the report.

But arguing about the details of the OR would get me nowhere, and in fact, would make me sound defensive and prickly. Instead, I decided that the best route for me to take was to firmly march down the road to program improvement. And the consultants had admirable ideas.

The OR was an impressive document that contained a new method of administrative accountability that seemed very smart. Unfortunately, their plan was costly: six new high-powered staff to man the fortress. I believed their not-so-hidden agenda was to wipe the slate clean.

The OR would require the surgical removal of my loyal team.

I found the consultants' vision both unrealistic and in opposition with my ethical standards. I thought about just flat-footedly stating that I wasn't terminating my staff. Instead, I decided, my team would have to be recognized by the dean's office as essential to the operation of my program.

Determined not to be negative, I hoped to convince the dean's office to compromise. I decided not to address the issue at the June 27 meeting with Roland and Shirley, as I thought it best to keep my idea under wraps for as long as possible.

The short meeting went well enough. In fact, Roland had found someone to temporarily work with me as a program manager. The new person, Vicki Skipper, was a retired management officer from another UC Davis department in the College of Innovations who was well-respected in the dean's office.

"You're going to like her," Roland told me, his deep blue eyes twinkling.

July 2007

On July 2, I met Vicki, a surprisingly young retiree with an engaging and friendly smile. We bonded immediately. She filled out the paperwork and gave it to the HR director that same day.

The next day, I met with the auditors, who went over their draft report with me: a number of crimes ($160,000 in travel fraud and equipment embezzlement) were attributed directly to Beverly. Other investigations regarding about $1 million in misappropriation of resources (such as using funds from a grant for nonapproved usages) found that expensive office renovations, computerized conference rooms, and hiring of staff to work in Raymond's laboratory were apparently approved by Beverly, for Raymond, without my knowledge. Luckily, the internal auditors found evidence that this was intentionally done behind my back.

Beverly, who had been indicted in March, continued to postpone her court appearance. I kept tabs on her using the federal court calendar, wondering when she'd have to face the music. (That day wouldn't arrive for another fifteen months!)

Vicki began working with me on July 11. I was amazed that she was hired faster than a speeding bullet! Of course, her connection with the dean's office made her a special hire. I organized a little brunch to welcome her to our program.

Vicki jumped right in. I could tell she was eager to help turn the program around and navigate us back to business. With her special connections and manager experience, she'd be able to organize the administration of the program in ways that Beverly never imagined!

No longer adrift, Vicki and I charted our new course. With Vicki Skipper at the helm, it was full steam ahead. No one was jumping ship on my watch!

On July 18, Vicki, Rebecca, and I reviewed our next year's plan. Our three-hundred-page submission included forty counties. The final step was the review of our updated funding proposal. I wanted our $13 million budget to be watertight. Two hours later we were done!

At noon, after clearing the decks, I took Rebecca and Vicki out to lunch to celebrate. At the restaurant, we were giddy with excitement. After paying the bill, I stepped outside to make a phone call.

Returning to the table ten minutes later, I overheard Vicki whispering to Rebecca. Vicki appeared to be suggesting to Rebecca that overtime was a good way to increase her salary.

"What I think you should do is figure out what the salary should be and record that in overtime hours," Vicki advised Rebecca.

Shocked, I blurted out to Vicki that Rebecca was required to get prior approval before she was allowed to work overtime. Vicki became quiet.

During the ride back to the office, I sat alone in the backseat. Vicki and Rebecca chatted as if they were best friends. I was reminded of Vicki's special relationship with the dean's office and wondered if her advice to Rebecca was some sort of test. Was Vicki trying to get Rebecca in trouble? Was this a ploy to discredit me?

Reporting Vicki's blunder to the folks who hired her would be tricky. The HR director, someone who barely spoke to me as it was, would hardly believe any criticism of her friend. Vicki, having been around the dean's office for years, would likely deny that she said anything inappropriate. I wasn't even sure if *verbal advice* to fraudulently use overtime would be considered a policy breach. But, although I wasn't happy making waves, I couldn't pretend it didn't happen.

One thing I did know: Rebecca was honest and wouldn't do anything to jeopardize her future. But having an authority figure from the dean's office advise this kind of wrongdoing couldn't help but be confusing. I needed to clarify for Vicki that I'd already preapproved Rebecca's overtime for the past week. Had Vicki heard some kind of gossip at the dean's office about Rebecca's telecommuting? I was worried. One thing that I'd learned over and over again, loose lips sink ships!

I planned to meet face to face with Vicki privately to discuss and correct her advice to Rebecca. That would be the most fair and reasonable approach and give Vicki the opportunity to explain.

Alas, the next morning Vicki left a message that she'd be out for two days. I put my plan to discuss the issue with her on hold.

I prepared a cover letter for our 2008 Food Stamp Education Plan and submitted it to the USDA with a copy to the dean's office. Later that afternoon, I received a positive response regarding our 2008 plan and budget request. There was just one hitch. The USDA had one final request, and it was a humdinger! I was asked to prepare a report on the university's response to the fraud!

I worked late into the night on that final inquiry, preparing a report entitled "University's Response to the Fraud." Because I quoted the OR in my draft, I expected the dean's office would be hard pressed to reject my draft. Although I was confident that my new program would be funded at $13 million come October 1st, I needed SEA Roland Babu to seal the deal.

I spent most of the next day, July 20th, finalizing my "Response to Fraud" report. It was a very hectic day spanning three cities: an early morning dental appointment in Berkeley, then up to Davis for a couple of meetings, and back to Oakland to join my daughter for our annual family picnic in Roberts Park.

Waiting for the tide to turn, I was on my best behavior. Now was not the time to rock the boat!

1 | **Entrapment**

August 13, 2007

It was the deadpan look on Percy's face that was my first clue. It was almost 1 p.m. on Monday, August 13, 2007, and I was waiting to meet with my supervisor, Dean Percy Grossman.

Twelve months had passed since I'd blown the whistle at UC Davis. As the director of a statewide program for low-income families, I'd been working like a dog to keep the program running under the watchful eyes of the dean's office at UC Davis.

I'd pretty much stayed away from my colleagues while I was waiting for the release of the fraud findings. I was confident that once my peers read the report they'd see for themselves that I'd been deceived by Beverly and her friend and ally, the chair of the department. Having served in the UC bureaucracy for almost three decades, I wasn't surprised that resolution was moving at a snail's pace.

My last hope was that Dean Grossman would swoop in and support me, as he'd done so many times in the not-so-distant past, as a sort-of-knight-in-shining-armor who would rise above the fray of dishonesty.

"Hi Percy," I said, looking up from my chair. I gave him a big smile and then jumped up to open the door as he entered

Rankor Hall, the home of the college dean's office. The College of Innovations was my new administrative abode.

My new boss, Percy Grossman, had finally returned from his overseas mission. He was a high-level dean at the University of California with years of experience consulting for international programs and counties all over the globe. A good friend, he'd frequently invited me into his home. But today, his usual friendly warm greeting was missing. Tall and a bit clumsy in his all-over neutral tan-sweater, khaki slacks, and brown suede loafers, his eyes looked straight ahead as he tried to maneuver his bicycle through the narrow doorway.

His bicycle clanged as it hit the metal frame and he said brusquely as he passed, "Be right with you."

"Don't worry, I'm early," I said, noticing that he was wearing clips on the bottom of his pants. One of them wasn't holding the leg properly, and bottom of his tan slacks was frayed and caked with dirt.

I'd been asked to meet with Percy by an assistant in his office. I read the assistant's email again as I looked at my watch; it was 1:10. I'd arrived early for the one o'clock meeting and found the office locked during the lunch hour. At 12:55 p.m. I was let into the waiting area.

The meeting didn't have an agenda, at least not one that was shared with me. I'd asked the assistant and was told that the meeting was just an update about my program. So I'd brought the organization chart with me to show that my office was still under-staffed.

Beverly Benford, the fraudster, had resigned on October 31, 2006. Before I blew the whistle, there were five employees (Beverly, Terrence, Rebecca, Ryan, and Ginny) working in my office.

Terrence was a new hire that I'd hoped would step in and help out. Instead, he'd bolted in January, without any notice! I assumed, after he took many days off from work, that he lacked the skill set to manage the office and was freaked out about the fraud.

When I made a routine request to fill both Beverly's and Terrence's positions, the HR director ignored my emails. Then, suddenly, the dean's office commissioned an organizational review. The OR, as I called it, was done by two consultants (retired accountants) who had come to my office and spent four hours meeting with me and my team.

The consultants were very friendly and sympathetic, giving us hope that things were about to get better. Their OR report was miraculous—with insightful and ambitious ideas. They envisioned a number of internal controls that would make Fort Knox look vulnerable. Clearly, fraud would never happen again.

In July the dean's office finally agreed to my request to fill Beverly's position. Vicki Skipper was hired on July 11, but found another position on campus two weeks later. I was back to square one and overwhelmed with work.

My only hope was to convince Percy that the vacant position urgently needed to be filled. However, there was one problem: the OR plan proposed a team of six new analysts! I'd done the math—we had funds to fill one job, not six.

I was concerned that my realistic appraisal wasn't going to be acceptable to the dean's office. They'd already hinted that they wanted me to terminate all my dedicated staff. Now wasn't the time to be negative. Despite my attempts to discuss realistic ideas, the dean's office wasn't happy. They weren't interested in a realistic plan; they wanted me to clean house.

I'd already promised myself I wasn't going to violate my own moral principles, even if it meant another fight with the powers that be. The OR, brilliant as it was, a masterful plan of efficiency, was really a plan that couldn't be implemented without wiping the slate clean. My team had worked very hard to get the program back in shape, and I wasn't going to terminate them—period!

So that day I'd brought with me a new plan to convince Percy that I would be able to hire a coordinator and keep my team. In addition, an article in the campus newspaper, the *California Aggie,* had sparked the attention of the legal folks at the USDA. I had drafted a response and wanted to get Percy to endorse it before sending.

Percy disappeared around the corner of the hallway with his bike hitting various partitions all way to his office. I returned to my chair and waited. A few minutes later, Shirley, the director of Human Resources walked past me and I said hello. Her lack of response was my second clue that something was up.

Shirley hadn't been returning my phone calls. I had been initially impressed with her when she told me that she'd been a private eye. At first, I recalled, she showed a bubbly enthusiasm when she talked about it, but when I asked a question, she suddenly became vague and changed the subject. I got the message that I appeared too interested. However, I still thought it was cool.

At the onset of the fraud investigation, I was told to work directly with Shirley. I found it difficult though, as she would tell me she was very busy. In the end, I dealt with her lack of response by documenting everything in writing. However, when she didn't respond to my email reporting that my office had been ransacked and I wanted to have the locks changed, I began to believe that she was avoiding me. Luckily, the case was turned over to the locally designated official (or LDO) for whistleblowers, who had responded promptly and effectively.

Percy came back to tell me that they were looking for a meeting room and that he'd return when one was found. This was my third clue: the need for a meeting room meant other people would be attending.

My watch said 1:20. A few minutes later I was told a room was found. Percy appeared and I followed him into the meeting room in the Human Resources area of the office. Shirley, bent over a computer in her office, was reserving the room and asked Percy for the time span. He said one hour.

The visiting academic dean, Lorenzo Maestro, arrived and sat down. On leave from his post at the University of Rome, Italy, he had a reputation for quick decisiveness. He was a tall, thin energetic man with an Abe Lincoln beard and long wispy hair, and although he looked like a conductor, with his jet-black hair, he was better known as an administrative guru—or in university lingo, a no-nonsense executive who received a big paycheck to handle difficult employment issues.

I sat down directly across from him. The room was very narrow, with a table and several chairs on either side. There was a water cooler with plastic cups at one end of the table and a blackboard at the other end.

Percy and Shirley came in and sat down. Percy asked Shirley to close the blinds on the window. "I don't want anyone pressing up on the glass to look in," he said.

"I'll be happy to make faces back at them," I replied trying to lighten the mood of the group. No one laughed.

Shirley got up and did as he asked. Dust from the blinds floated through the air. Lorenzo had changed chairs, and she asked him if she could sit on his right side. He nodded.

I wondered if she wanted to sit there because he was left-handed. As I watched him pull out his notebook, I could see that he had a page of handwritten notes. I glanced at the upside-down page. It was Percy's handwriting!

While Lorenzo was reading the notes, I noted Shirley shifting in her chair.

"I have a quick question about the article in *California Aggie* that sparked a legal question from the USDA," I said to fill the void.

They all looked up and stared at me. Lorenzo cleared his throat, and said that he'd begin the meeting in a minute. It was more than a little strange that he was conducting the meeting. Percy, sitting on my left was uncomfortably sprawled all over his chair and facing the wall.

"We have asked you here today to discuss a serious matter," was Lorenzo's first sentence. What he said next was the shocker!

"Vicki Skipper, one of our most valued and leading management employees from the college worked in your office for only two weeks. During our routine exit interview with her, she said that her resignation was prompted by a recent meeting with you. She told us that you became very angry, rose out of your chair, and began to shout at her for fifteen minutes. She said that you became so animated and agitated and when you stood above her and raised your arm, she feared you would strike her."

For a terrifying moment, I felt the palpitations in my heart giving way to a severe flash of light, followed by a stab of pain as the room got narrower. I then felt the rush of adrenaline moving throughout my heart as though I'd just drunk six cups of coffee.

"That didn't happen." I said quickly, wondering how loud my voice was sounding—the room seemed to be spinning. I wanted to stand up and call her a liar—but I managed to hold back and contain myself.

"She's incorrect," I said squarely.

"She said she resigned because of your intimidating and threatening behavior. She said that she tried to be conciliatory by making some suggestions to you, but that you were enraged," Lorenzo said without missing a beat.

"Vicki is one of our leading management officers and we have the highest confidence in her," he repeated. "Your yelling and demanding answers is against university policy. In fact, I must call your attention to the policy that addresses 'violence, threats, and disruption in the workplace,'" he added.

The silence was deafening. I managed to maintain eye contact with Lorenzo. I paused to take in some oxygen and asked, "When did she say this happened?"

"Our exit interview was about ten days ago," was the answer I received. He was obviously avoiding my question.

Lorenzo soberly stared at me, waiting. I sat frozen wondering why he was in charge of the meeting. Who is this guy? I didn't even know him!

The three of them remained silent. I could barely think. In my head, I quickly subtracted ten days from August 13th and got August 3rd. I was puzzled. There wasn't any meaning to the date. I started to babble just to keep my head above water.

"August 3rd was ten days ago. Vicki quit in July. I believe her last day was July 25th, the day I was in Fresno. I received a telephone call from my office informing me that she'd quit. I didn't even know that she was planning on quitting."

I wondered if I was talking loud enough for them to hear me. My voice sounded far away to me, but I maintained eye contact, holding my head up.

I gripped the table to pull myself forward to get a better look at Lorenzo. In the back of my mind, I visualized my calendar, beginning to recall those two short weeks that Vicki worked in my office. I planted my feet firmly on the floor to sit upright.

Suddenly, a meeting with Vicki in late July began to take shape. I'd met with her on Monday, July 23rd. Vicki had advised Rebecca, one of my staff, to submit overtime hours to increase her salary. This could be a violation of university policy and I'd told her so. I didn't recall that she was even slightly upset when we met.

"I do recall meeting with Vicki. But I didn't yell or scream at her," I answered forcefully.

I began to piece together my meeting with Vicki. She'd committed a kind-of policy breach the week before, and I'd met with her to discuss it. I then followed up the meeting by sending her an email to document our discussion. I thought I'd handled it well by asking Vicki to correct the inappropriate advice she'd given to Rebecca. I recalled Vicki sounding remorseful. It was really weird—I was mystified why Vicki would advise Rebecca to use overtime to increase her salary.

Now I thought differently. Yes, Vicki must have been very upset about that meeting when I called into question her inappropriate behavior. Even though she was very apologetic and promised to correct her mistake immediately, she must have been furious! This must have triggered her false accusation.

At the time, I couldn't understand why Vicki would suggest such nonsense to Rebecca. No one would walk into an office that was being scrutinized by the U.S. Attorney and commit a policy breach. Who'd take such a risk? Was this some sort of trick by the dean's office to get me in trouble?

I managed not to convey of any of my speculations out loud. Instead, I pressed on for details and wrote down what was happening. I'd need the details to defend myself.

"I met with Vicki on July 23rd. Is this the meeting you're referring to?" I asked calmly.

I looked directly at Lorenzo who was staring right back at me with dagger eyes.

He ignored my question completely. He then made a statement that he repeated over and over again.

"Vicki is an outstanding employee; we have every confidence in her" was said again and again. I made six checkmarks to note the number of times he made this statement.

"We're willing to forget about this incident, if you admit to it now," Lorenzo said shrilly. I watched Shirley stiffen as he encouraged me to "take the offer." "*All of this will go away,*" I heard him add, his voice warbling.

"You should seriously consider the alternatives!" Lorenzo demanded, reaching a falsetto high note.

I could hardly say no thank you, to something totally false as well as unethical. When did the dean's office get to act like the police? Was Dean Maestro trying to orchestrate the end of my career?

"I didn't yell or scream at Vicki. I didn't raise my arm to strike her."

"You are attempting to derail our meeting," Lorenzo said gruffly. They tried to coax me into providing an explanation. Lorenzo was very stern. His tone was increasingly sharp, and he never wavered on his desire to get me to confess.

I was taken aback that Lorenzo was conducting a discussion on accusations that he appeared to have little knowledge about. What had Vicki told them? Why was Lorenzo in charge? What was Percy doing?

The calendar in my head was now clear and I recalled that I documented the meeting, and that I'd sent my email to both Vicki and Percy! I'd sent that email right after my meeting with Vicki on July 23rd.

"Vicki violated university policy," I began and carefully watched their responses. They revealed nothing.

"I met with her on July 23rd and followed our meeting up with an email to her and to your office," I added. "The email is dated July 23rd. Is this the meeting that you're talking about?" I asked calmly.

Lorenzo responded quickly: "No, not July 23rd."

"Then when?" I pressed. I believed that they actually knew about Vicki's mistake and all of this was just to turn the tables on me and cover up her blunder.

"July 20th," Percy announced with staid irritation.

"July 20th?" I repeated. "There must be some mistake. I met with Vicki on Monday. July 20th was Friday, and …"

Then, as if I'd been struck by lightning, I recalled that I had seen Vicki briefly on Friday. She had abruptly stormed into my office that day, waving an envelope at me, and was quite agitated, which made me nervous.

"As I recall, Vicki was out of the office on Friday July 20th. In the late afternoon, she did stop by, but we didn't …" I decided not to mention her barging into my office with a tobacco-colored envelope. I didn't know what was in the envelope—she never gave it to me—but I recognized it as the type used by the dean's office when I'd been served at my home in Kensington.

"That was it," Lorenzo said quickly interrupting me. As I sat there stunned, I began to recall that my assessment of Vicki changed radically after she behaved so rudely. Her previous polite and admiring comments to me about my courageous act as a whistleblower had really won me over. Her waving that envelope at me was contrary to her formerly friendly demeanor. I'd assumed by her charging into my office and the irate expression on her face that she was the bearer of more bad news.

"She came in," I began. "I was writing a report for the USDA on the university's response to the fraud. You may recall, Percy," I said with more confidence, "that I sent you a draft of the University's Response to Fraud that afternoon to review. I told Vicki we'd meet on Monday, July 23rd."

I recalled that I was trying to finish this complex report so I could get out of my office by 5:00 to join my daughter at our picnic in the Oakland hills.

The report was the key to our getting funding for the next year. I'd been asked to provide in writing the steps that the university was going to take to eliminate the fraud. This was essentially the only item standing in the way of getting next year's funding approved. I thought the draft I wrote would be easily endorsed by the university, since I'd used the dean's office OR report to prepare it.

"You screamed and yelled at her for fifteen minutes," Lorenzo said sternly. "You raised your arm as if to strike her!" he added with a crescendo.

"No, that didn't happen," I said warily, and added. "You can talk to my staff about that. They will be able to tell you that there was no yelling in my office. Vicki was there for maybe five minutes," I said.

Shirley had begun writing but stopped and watched. She glanced at Lorenzo who was staring at me.

I looked him in the eyes and said evenly and slowly: "I didn't scream, I didn't yell, I didn't rise out of my chair, and I didn't raise my arm."

"So what do you do when you are angry?" Lorenzo asked.

"I've had employees yell at me," I said recalling Beverly's tirades, "and I've asked them to leave my office and calm down. My usual response to anger is to take notes and then follow up with an email.

"The meeting I had with Vicki was on July 23rd. I sent her an email following our meeting," I said hoping for a nod. "Did Vicki show you my July 23rd email?"

No reply.

Then I remembered something else I'd done.

"Before I met with Vicki, I called the provost's office and left a voicemail that I was going to have to write up an incident. I left that message on Sunday, July 22nd."

I didn't tell the dean's office that I left a voicemail message about Vicki's policy breach for the provost's office because I believed the dean's office was reading my emails.

Percy finally spoke.

"Your denial is a big part of your problem. Others have reported similar things."

"Similar?" I asked startled. "What do you mean?"

"Yelling and screaming. Threatening and intimidating," Percy suddenly seemed angry.

"Who said that?" I asked mystified.

"I have written statements from at least three people," he replied.

"Who?" I asked.

"That's confidential," Percy replied harshly.

"I believe you're required to inform me of allegations and I have the right to respond to them," I answered quickly.

"Terry," he announced. "She filed a grievance against you."

"Who's Terry?" I asked, looking around the room.

"Percy, her name isn't Terry," said Lorenzo, trying to get Percy's attention. "That newbie in your office who quit in January," he stated looking at me.

"Oh," I said thinking out loud. "You mean Terrence? He's a guy."

I was startled that Terrence, of all people, had filed a grievance. He was a new employee that began a few weeks before I blew the whistle. He'd bolted immediately after that.

"If Terrence filed a grievance against me, I wasn't informed," I said. "Terrence left six months ago," I added. "I'd like to see a copy of his grievance."

No response.

"And the other two people, did they also file a grievance?" I asked, knowing full well that my personnel file was completely free of any complaints.

Percy suddenly started talking.

"Vicki said that you were angry and told her that you weren't going to implement the OR," Percy snapped.

"We didn't talk about the OR!"

"You told Vicki that the OR report made you look like an *ass!*" Percy added crassly.

"I didn't say that!" I was shocked by his choice of words. "Again, we never discussed the OR."

I pressed on, deciding now was the time to tell them why Vicki would be so upset and make up this story.

"Vicki told Rebecca to use overtime to increase her salary," I told them. "Vicki's advice to use overtime was inappropriate, and I asked her to send Rebecca an email with correct information on use of overtime.

"Vicki agreed with this plan to send Rebecca an email. I wrote up our discussion of the incident," I said recalling the details more clearly. "In fact," I added with confidence, "your office was copied on my email," I looked at Percy, watching for a nod of agreement. He turned his head away.

"Did Vicki show you the email correction she sent to Rebecca?" I asked.

No one said a word.

"Vicki wrote a very clear email admitting her mistake. She wrote to Rebecca that her suggestion was against university policy," I finished. Expecting that this would end their allegations about Vicki's claim, I assumed that they'd read Vicki's email. Were they hoping I'd forgotten about it?

"I really doubt that Vicki would do that," Lorenzo concluded with a snarl of sarcasm.

"You should ask Rebecca," I said writing this down in my notes. "Rebecca and others in my office are really overwhelmed," I stated. "There's a lot of work to do and it's been difficult," I added. "First, Terrence leaves, then Vicki," I said. "I was worried that Rebecca would leave as well.

"As a concerned supervisor I sought assistance from ASAP to try to get some help before Rebecca and my other staff burned out. They were all suffering from anxiety and stress."

ASAP, the Academic and Staff Assistance Program, was our university program that offered support for employees and supervisors on a range of issues.

Percy glared at me. "You met with ASAP?"

"Yes," I said with renewed confidence, "I met with ASAP to help my staff cope with the investigative process and workload," I said.

Percy turned in his chair to face me. I saw the "gotcha" moment blazing across his face.

He bolted upright and cocked his head in my direction. He gave me a questioning look that spelled trouble. Suddenly, I felt the need to make sure that he knew I was telling the truth.

I opened my purse, sitting on the chair next to me, and took out my appointment book. I pulled out the card that I was given by the assistant director of ASAP with the two dates and times we met marked by him on his card.

"I'm unhappy that I feel the need to prove to you that I had confidential conversations with the ASAP assistant director about my staff members," I said, handing the card to Percy. "I met with him because of my desire to help my staff. I wasn't seeking mental health treatment for myself," I added.

He turned his head away, and I noted his upper lip was trembling as if in an internal rage. He was obviously upset.

He handed the card to Shirley, who looked at it, then at me. She handed it back. Lorenzo was staring at the notes and wasn't even paying attention.

Then as suddenly as it began, the meeting was over. I asked if they were putting Vicki's allegation in writing.

"No," said Percy shaking his head back and forth.

Although I wanted to feel relief, I was skeptical. This meeting's purpose was to get me to confess and they hadn't succeeded.

We all stood up. Percy walked over to the water cooler in the back of the room. He took a plastic cup from the dispenser. He bent over and pushed down on the lever to fill his cup. For some reason, it wasn't working. I went over to provide some expert assistance.

"Sometimes it helps just to kick it," I said smiling and pushing the large water tank back and forth. Suddenly, water poured into his cup and onto the floor.

"Oops!" I said, as I opened the conference room door and walked out. "Your cup runneth over …"

2 | **Documentation**

After that dreadful meeting, I returned to my office and began creating a timeline of my entire relationship with Vicki. The timeline could help me to figure out what was going on. Why would Vicki Skipper turn on me?

Booting up my computer, I believed the answers would be found in the two critical emails from July 23. The first was my email to Vicki about our meeting. The second was Vicki's email to Rebecca.

On July 23rd, I'd sent a very long and detailed email to Vicki right after our 1:00 discussion. As I'd recalled correctly in the meeting with Lorenzo and Percy, I'd copied the dean's office on this email:

> Dear [Vicki],
>
> I am very pleased that you are providing guidance … When we met on July 18, you had some good ideas … I need to document that today we have discussed … During our lunch meeting … you requested to [Rebecca] that she should put in overtime hours even if she did not work those hours … You told her to calculate an acceptable salary level and then determine how many overtime hours she

would need to be paid to get that amount ... This request does not adhere to University policy ... [Rebecca] can only report hours she actually worked ... and were pre-approved by me ... You told me that you would ... explain to [Rebecca] the correct policy ...

Vicki's email to Rebecca, sent twenty-five minutes later, was even better than my email documenting our discussion. It included in the subject line "A correction and apology":

During our lunch meeting with Amy Joy, I made a statement to you that is incorrect and does not follow policy. I want to be clear that you may only claim overtime that is pre-approved by Amy Joy. This is University policy ...

Vicki provided evidence of her misdeed using her own words! She hadn't copied the dean's office, so I assumed that Vicki hadn't mentioned this email during her exit interview.

I entered the information onto my timeline:

July 23:

1:00 p.m. Met with Vicki for thirty minutes to discuss inappropriate advice to Rebecca. She apologized and agreed to correct her misinformation.

1:43 p.m. Sent email to Vicki to document incident and discussion with Vicki on how to correct it. I copied dean's office on my email to Vicki.

2:08 p.m. Vicki sent correction/apology email to Rebecca. Vicki copied me on her email to Rebecca.

After concluding that I had sufficient documentation that Vicki had admitted and corrected her mistake, I then turned to the date that the dean's office had said the alleged incident took place, July 20th. Did Vicki get the dates mixed up?

July 20th was easily recalled. Starting the day with a dental appointment in Berkeley at 8 a.m., I'd traveled to three different cities.

I had sixty-six emails on my computer dated July 20. I printed only the emails that could be verified as ones I had sent. There were twenty-eight.

In fact, I'd sent an email to Vicki in the late afternoon. I noted on the timeline that Vicki wasn't in the office on July 20th.

As my printer hummed, I heard my staff next door laughing. I was well aware that my office had thin walls. During the investigation, my staff told me that Beverly was always shushing everyone in the office so she could listen to my phone calls through the wall.

As I added information to the timeline, I could see that I'd spent most of the day sending drafts of my "University's Response to the Fraud" report to various campus dignitaries.

An email that I'd sent to Ginny documented a meeting with her from 3:30 to 4:00 p.m. We'd spent the time preparing an eight-page purchase order that I faxed at 4 p.m. I found the fax and the fax confirmation report documenting that it was sent at 4:02. My next email was a short email to the vice-provost at 4:10 about an article that featured his work at Davis. At 4:20 I sent a document that was to be discussed at my 4:30 meeting that day. Around 5:00, I dashed to my car to get to the picnic in Oakland.

As I filled in the activities of July 20th, a wave of nostalgia took me by surprise. July 20, coincidentally, was my wedding anniversary, though my husband, Leonard, had moved out long before. I was greatly relieved that he had no knowledge of any of this!

July 20:

8:00 a.m. Dentist appointment in Berkeley.

8:45 a.m. Emailed 1st draft of "University's Response to Fraud" to the dean's office from my home in Kensington.

10:30 a.m. Arrived at Davis. Revised 1st draft.

1:15 p.m. Emailed 2nd draft for review. Revised 2nd draft.

2:11 p.m. Email 3rd draft for review.

3:23 p.m. Sent email to Vicki. She wasn't in the office.

3:30–4:00 p.m. Met with Ginny about curriculum order.

4:02 p.m. Faxed order to vendor and received confirmation.

4:09 p.m. Sent email to VP. He replied at 4:15 p.m.

4:20 p.m. Emailed Strategic Plan for 4:30 p.m. meeting.

4:30 p.m. Strategic Plan meeting.

5:00 p.m. Left UC Davis for Oakland.

Reviewing the timeline, I guessed that Vicki burst into my office sometime after 4:20. The timeline made it clear that she could have only been in my office for about five minutes.

Searching for more clues, I traced the entire history of my relationship with Vicki from July 2 when I met her in Shirley's office. I detailed our relationship from July 2 to August 13:

> **July 2, 2007** Vicki and I met at the dean's office at 3:30 p.m. I had the feeling she was a good friend of Shirley Handover, the HR director.

> **July 11** Vicki began on Wednesday at 1:00 p.m. I had a staff meeting to introduce her to everyone and a brunch to welcome her.

> **July 12** Vicki worked with Ginny and Ryan. I met with Rebecca to discuss next year's budget. Rebecca and I met with Roland later in the day.

> **July 13** Vicki called in sick. She's out for 3 days.

> **July 18** Rebecca and I met with Vicki to review the final budget. I took Vicki and Rebecca out to lunch in Davis. Rebecca drove us to the restaurant. After lunch, I overheard Vicki advising Rebecca to use overtime to increase her UC Davis salary.

> **July 19** Vicki was out of the office all day. I prepared the first draft of the "University's Response to Fraud" at home using the dean's office OR.

> **July 20** I had a dental appointment in Berkeley at 8:00 a.m. I sent the first draft of the report to Roland at 8:45 a.m. then drove to

Davis. I arrived at UC Davis around 10:30 a.m. I sent the next draft at 1:15 p.m., then another version at 2:11 p.m. Of the 28 emails I sent that day, one was to Vicki, at 3:23 p.m., who wasn't in the office. Sometime after 4:20 p.m. Vicki burst into my office for about five minutes.

July 22 On Sunday afternoon I left a voice-mail message with an official at the provost's office that I'm going to discuss a policy breach with a staff member on Monday.

July 23 I met with Vicki at 1:00 p.m. and we discussed the incident. She wasn't upset. I asked her to correct the misinformation that she told Rebecca. Vicki agreed to send Rebecca an email to apologize for and cor-rect her inappropriate advice. I followed up our meeting with an email to Vicki and cop-ied the dean's office. My one-page email was written to document the incident and the steps I took to correct it.

July 24 Vicki worked at home all day.

July 25 At 5:00 a.m. I drove to Fresno for an all-day site visit. Sometime during the day, Vicki announces it's her last day.

Delving into her last day, I recalled the Ginny called me in Fresno at the end of the day to give me some news.

"Guess who announced her last day?" Ginny said to me on the telephone. Without waiting for an answer, she burst out with "Vicki!"

"You're kidding," I said stunned and horrified. "What happened?"

"This afternoon, we were all meeting with Vicki to go over the staff manual," Ginny reminded me.

"Vicki handed me her copy of the manual and said she'd made some handwritten comments for you." Ginny continued, "She then turned to the group and announced that today was her last day."

"Everyone sat there stunned," Ginny added. "Vicki then said she enjoyed meeting everyone."

"Whoa," I said really shocked. "Did she say why?"

"I asked her," Ginny told me. "She indicated she had another campus job. I asked her if you knew she was leaving," Ginny said. "She said that she'd already told you."

"Well, she didn't," I said matter-of-factly. "Maybe she left me a note or her timesheet in my mail box," I added, expecting that she'd communicated her decision to me directly.

"Hold on," Ginny said and put the telephone down. "There's nothing in your mail box," she said after checking my office.

"Isn't Vicki supposed to give two weeks' notice?" Ginny asked.

"Yep," I answered. "This must be some kind of record," I said, annoyed. "She couldn't give two weeks' notice. She only worked a few days!"

I edited my July 25 entry to include my recollection of Ginny's phone call: "At around 5:00 p.m., Ginny called to tell me that Vicki announced she took another position on campus."

In fact, Vicki had sent her goodbye email to Rebecca! Rebecca shared Vicki's swan song with me the next day:

> Hi [Rebecca], I have accepted another position on campus. It was my pleasure to meet you and learn more about what you have done and are doing. This is my last afternoon … Warmly, [Vicki]"

I added this information for July 25.

July 25 At 5:00 a.m. I drove to Fresno for an all-day site visit. Sometime during the day, Vicki announces it's her last day to the office staff. At around 5:00 p.m., Ginny called to tell me that Vicki announced she took another position on campus. Vicki told Rebecca that July 25 was her last day. Rebecca was really bummed!

Neither Rebecca nor I had any inkling that Vicki was upset. We all assumed that Vicki couldn't weather the storm—whether it was the drama of the investigation or a feeling the ship was sinking. I wasn't able to find out anything from the powers that be.

July 26 Back at UCD, I called Shirley to find out what happened with Vicki. No one responded. I signed Vicki's timesheet.

July 27 I took Vicki's timesheet over to the dean's office hoping to speak directly with Shirley. I was told that no one was available to meet with me. I left her timesheet with the dean's office assistant.

Looking for additional clues, I read all my emails following Vicki's departure. It was a rather eerie to write "nothing" on my time line until August 8.

July 30–August 7 Nothing.

August 8 Percy's assistant had set up a meeting with Percy for 1:00 p.m. on August 13 to discuss the 2008 submission. She sent an email.

August 13 Meeting with Percy along with Lorenzo and Shirley at 1:00 p.m. The meeting began at 1:20 p.m.

———

I heard a knock at my office door. It was approaching 4:30 p.m.

"Come in," I said turning to the door. Ryan, our tech guy, walked in. He handed me a binder that contained a printed copy of our 2008 Plan.

"Here it is!" he said proudly. "It's really heavy," he indicated as I held out both my hands to collect the binder.

"Thanks!" I said smiling looking down at my copy. The three-hundred-page document was our Food Stamp Education Plan for 2008. "Do you think anyone's gonna read it?"

"Can't miss the cool front cover," Ryan answered, grinning.

I'd included everyone's name and contribution on the front cover. This was the first year that teamwork played a big role in getting things fixed. We'd become a close-knit crew, fiercely committed to putting our program back on the map!

Ten minutes later, I finished my timeline. Confident that I could prove the dean's office's allegations were false, I called Vice-Chancellor Franklin Taylor-Starr, the LDO for whistleblowers. I wanted to report the issue directly to Frank and get his guidance on what to do about it.

"Hi Frank," I began, "I know it's almost five but I was hoping to talk to you for a few minutes."

"Hi Amy," he said. "Sure, what can I do for you?" he answered.

"I need to tell you about another incident," I said, warming up. "I had a meeting at the dean's office this afternoon, and they have verbally reported some serious allegations from a former employee," I told him.

"Hmm ...," he said, pausing. "I have *some* knowledge of these issues," he told me. He managed to make the word *some* sound really dark.

"I was hoping that I could get some guidance from you on how to handle the situation," I said, getting right to the heart of the matter.

"Amy," he said pointedly, "I'm unable to advise you regarding this ... ahh ... issue," he finished.

This was the first time ever that he told me that he was unable to provide guidance. I was startled.

In a wave of panic, I imagined my $13 million program with *someone else* at the helm! Now that I succeeded in getting the USDA to restore funding for my UC Davis program, the dean's office was done with me. Was their plan to toss me overboard?

Driving home, I became aware of something that I hadn't considered. Starting with Beverly, then Raymond, followed by Fred—their denial, anger, and rage about getting caught was predictable.

But now, with Percy and Lorenzo making waves, I started to wonder. Wouldn't the dean's office want to safe guard the person who'd helped the university stop fraud? Isn't that why the university moved me to the dean's office in the first place?

Was *this* the university's response to my exposing criminal activity? I'd read these kinds of stories from others who'd blown the whistle on something much more scary—corruption.

Pure and simple: this retaliation was meant to *hurt me*.

August 14, 2007

The next day, August 14, I decided I wanted concrete answers. I'd asked the dean's office to check with Rebecca about her interaction with Vicki on July 18th. Now it was my turn to find out about that lunch meeting.

"[Rebecca]," my email began, "I have been asked by the dean's office [some questions regarding our] Wednesday, July 18th ... lunch meeting with [Vicki Skipper] at Café Italio ... Do you recall that day?"

Rebecca, in her usual honest and unflappable style, responded right away. After some introductory comments about the stress from the excessive workload, she responded with a yes, she did recall July 18:

> [Vicki] suggested the following, and I can give direct quotes: "OK, now [Roland] would probably kill me for saying this but what I think you should do is figure out what the position would make and record that in OT [over time] hours."

Rebecca then added her own perspective on the lunch encounter:

> I think I said "OK" and my mind was a bit spinning because our group has been on such a roller coaster ... I was so happy to have someone ... I thought could really help and be a resource ... proverbial life jacket ... took me by surprise as it's counter to what I would have expected from someone at that level ... it was ... weird.

I was more than pleased with Rebecca's direct quotes.

Vicki Skipper must have become furious after I reported her to the dean's office. Did she make up this allegation to avoid getting into hot water? And the dean's office would be more than happy to give me the heave-ho now that our funding was secure!

August 16, 2007

On Thursday, August 16, I received a calendar request from Percy to discuss programmatic connections. There was no email about the meeting this time—it was just put on my dean's office calendar. The meeting was set for 9:00 a.m. on Friday, August 17. I wasn't even sure what a "programmatic connection" was, although I was fairly sure that this wasn't good news.

When I arrived for the meeting at the dean's office, I was first asked to sit in the waiting room and then escorted to Lorenzo's office, where both he and Percy were waiting. Lorenzo handed me one of those brown envelopes.

I opened the envelope to find a single-spaced eight-page letter signed by Lorenzo and copied to Percy, Roland, and Shirley. Lorenzo motioned me to a chair nearby. It was entitled "Summary of our August 13th meeting"; Lorenzo told me to read it.

The date of the letter was August 15. I ignored the icy stares of the two deans seated inches away from me. As I sat down in the chair, I planted my feet firmly on the ground. I was fully prepared to weather any storm.

> The purpose of this letter is to memorialize key aspects of and agreements derived at our meeting of 13 August ...

> ... In an exit interview, [Vicki] said that her resignation was prompted by a recent meeting that she had with you ...

> ... [Vicki] said that you immediately became very angry, rose up out of your chair, and began shouting at her ... saying the report was terrible, that it made you look like an ass and that you had no intention of implementing it. She said that you became so agitated and animated that she feared that she might be struck ...

As I read the letter, I noted immediately that there was no mention of a date for this alleged encounter. I assumed that this was done intentionally. Vicki had created a way to explain her sudden departure. Did she think that her false claim could erase what she'd done on July 18?

> ...You, on the other hand, indicated that the meeting with [Vicki] was not about the [OR] ... Rather, you wanted to address a concern you had about some information that [Vicki] allegedly gave to [Rebecca] at a recent lunch attended by the three of you ...

I noted that they used the word *alleged* in the sentence about Vicki's advice to Rebecca. Did they even speak to Rebecca?

The letter contained several positive comments about Ms. Skipper: "...we had the highest confidence in [Vicki] ... leading [manager] in the College ... impeccable credentials ..."

As I reached the end of the letter, more unsubstantiated hearsay was included:

> ... what she described to us regarding your verbal, threatening confrontation bore similarities to ... two [county colleagues] ... had [told Percy of] verbal abuse ...

The letter was devoid of facts. No dates, no names, no specific events. Did they think their private meetings, hearsay, innuendos, gossip, and false accusations would intimidate me?

A serious allegation on the last page signaled danger: Violence in the Workplace. Vicki gave the dean's office exactly what they'd been looking for: a plan to discredit my character and integrity.

This retaliation was personal.

I looked up from the letter and asked Percy one question: "When did this alleged incident take place?"

"July 20th," Percy answered.

"What time?"

"In the afternoon," he replied.

The meeting ended. Lorenzo gave his marching orders. "I need to have your written response by August 31, 2007," he drummed.

Clearly, if I hadn't prepared and saved an elaborate minute-by-minute paper trail to document the facts, I'd be up the creek. The dean's office was hoping that I'd surrender to their pirate ploy and walk the plank.

Nothing could be further from the truth.

3 | Michael A. Hirst, Esq.

After the meeting, I walked to my car in the parking lot to call, Michael A. Hirst, the former Supervisory Assistant U.S. Attorney, whose practice was devoted to representing whistleblowers. I'd consulted him earlier, during the original fraud investigation.

The dean's letter contained a serious allegation that could end my career at the university and damage my reputation. After the August 13 meeting with Lorenzo and Percy, I'd assumed that Vicki had filed a grievance, but this was something much more serious.

I was well versed in resolving personnel issues regarding staff, so my timeline was prepared to defeat a personnel complaint from Vicki. However, with two powerful deans and the HR director asserting that their employee's story was truthful, this would escalate their charges. In addition, the dean's office was alleging that there were other complainants who'd voiced similar wrongdoing. They were doing this to illustrate a pattern of violent behavior.

This kind of character assassination and reputation destruction required a different strategy. And with only two weeks to reply to their letter, I needed an expert.

"Hello, Mr. Hirst," I began. "My name is Amy Block Joy. I'm the whistleblower from the University of California," I said when he answered the telephone.

"I blew the whistle on fraud a year ago. Today I received a letter that threatens my future at the university. I'm hoping I can meet with you to discuss retaliation," I added.

"Hello, Amy," Michael said. "I remember our earlier discussion about your whistleblower case," he added. "Please call me Michael, and tell me what's going on."

"I've been falsely accused of workplace violence," I stated. "The letter says that I've threatened and intimidated an employee. I did not threaten her—or anyone for that matter."

"Vicki is her name ... Vicki Skipper. She made the whole thing up," I added, feeling at a loss for words. "The allegations have been included in a letter from two powerful deans," I said trying to be concise. "One of them is my boss," I whispered. "And the other ... ahh ... might be ... invincible!"

"Where are you now?" Michael asked.

"I'm calling you from my car at UC Davis. Five minutes ago," I said talking more softly as someone walked past me to get to their car, "I was handed a letter. The two deans, Percy Grossman and Lorenzo Maestro watched me read it."

I read him the part of the letter that addressed the accusations from Vicki. When I got to the sentence that describes the alleged threat against her, I could barely speak.

"'...you immediately became very angry, rose up out of your chair, and began shouting at her ... saying the report was terrible, that it made you look like an ass and that you had no intention of implementing it. She said that you became so agitated and animated that she feared that she might be struck.'

"Vicki made all this up," I asserted.

"What's the date of the alleged incident?" he asked.

"Vicki said it happened on Friday, July 20," I answered. "She popped into my office on July 20th for about five minutes," I said. "There's some sort of mix-up, since I met with

Vicki on July 23rd, not the 20th. Vicki had committed a policy breach the week before, and I met with her for about thirty minutes to discuss it."

"What kind of policy breach?" Michael asked.

"Vicki had advised one of my staff members—her name is Rebecca—to use overtime to increase her salary.

"I documented the meeting and the breach, including her admitting her mistake," I told him. "And Vicki wrote an email of correction," I added with some elation. "Vicki is either mixed up or thinks her false accusations will erase the advice she gave Rebecca."

"Go ahead," Michael said, "I'm following."

"Vicki was hired by the dean's office to help me, and then left after only two weeks. Actually five working days!" I added, "I didn't yell at her. I didn't scream. I didn't threaten her," I said adamantly. "What she said isn't true!"

"Let me see if I understand," Michael began. "You're saying that Vicki made a policy mistake, and after you confronted her about it she quit. Now she's falsely accused you of threatening her?"

"Yes, that's what happened."

"Could you fax me the letter and anything else you think might be helpful?" he asked, and then gave me his fax number.

"I'll fax you the dean's office letter and my documentation," I promised.

"OK. If the timing works for you, let's plan to meet on Wednesday, August 29th at 9:30 a.m."

After saying goodbye, I walked quickly to my office and turned on my computer. I wanted to see if the dean's office had made any more demands to see me. They hadn't.

Sitting quietly at my desk, I printed a second copy of my timeline and read it again. Relieved that I'd prepared written documentation before getting the allegations, I tried to read their letter a second time. When I got to their first statement about how wonderful Vicki was, I put the letter back into the envelope and into my briefcase.

I found some relief in looking at my daughter's high school graduation photo on my desk. She'd been accepted at UCLA. I was so excited that she was about to embark on the whole college experience. I was driving her down to Los Angeles on September 20th.

I looked at my August calendar. Egad! My response to the dean's office was due in two weeks—that would be Friday, August 31st!

It was now lunchtime, but I didn't feel like eating. I heard a knock on my door.

"Come in," I said trying to snap out of my funk.

Ryan Holt, my IT guy, peeked into my office and said he had some good news.

"Great to see you, Ryan," I said eager to hear some good news.

"I've printed a picture of our new home page for the website for you to review," Ryan said as handed me a copy. "We're ready to launch the new site!"

Looking down at the page he handed me, I motioned for him to take a seat in my office. He'd created a collage of some photographs I'd collected over the years. I'd asked colleagues to send some program snapshots for use in PowerPoint presentations.

"Wow!" I said, smiling at Ryan.

Illustrating the ethnic diversity, as well as the food habits of good health, the photos captured the unique message about our program. Ryan had composed a colorful display of close-ups: families with young children in the kitchen helping their moms and dads prepare a casserole full of healthy vegetables; a mom shopping at a farmer's market with her two young toddlers munching on organic carrots; a dad and a daughter creating a homemade fruit smoothie; and my personal favorite, a group of an extended-family from different generations talking, laughing, and enjoying their meal to-gether.

His collage was joyous! Research has shown that the health of children, both physically and emotionally, is better when family-like groups share the eating experience.

Even more enchanting was a close-up photo of a ten-month-old baby captured in a moment of pure delight—holding onto a spoon for the first time!

"Ryan," I said looking at him, "this is wonderful!"

I felt better. Focusing on the future of my program helped to get me anchored to what really mattered. I wasn't going to let the dean's office stop my program in their efforts to crush me.

Before leaving for home that afternoon, I wrote a short email individually to each of my team asking if they'd been contacted by the dean's office regarding Vicki's departure on July 25th. Since I'd asked the dean's office to consult with them about what happened, I wanted to find out if they had.

I received responses right away! Not a single member of my office had been contacted by anyone from the dean's office. Most of my team just responded with a no, but one wrote, "Nope. Nada from the bigwigs. By the way, who's Vicki?"

August 18–20, 2007

On Saturday, August 18, after a good night's sleep, I started preparing my response to the dean's office's letter. I decided that my best line of defense would be my already prepared timeline, but I wanted Michael to review everything that I'd documented regarding the event.

I typed a short introductory paragraph. I decided to re-type the dean's office's letter verbatim under my introduction. I then separated out each of their allegations and numbered them consecutively. When I was done with the numbering, I had fifteen allegations. Of the fifteen, seven were career-ending: violence, threats, intimidation, yelling, shouting, using force, and workplace disruptions.

Their letter also implied that I'd lied about Vicki's advice to Rebecca and forced Vicki to write a letter of apology! There were a number of unspecific accusations about my demeanor with Vicki and others, including anger, using foul language, verbal threats, and intimidation.

I responded to each allegation using a red font. I wanted Michael to have all the facts. I spent an hour working on my draft.

Dear [Deans Maestro and Grossman]:

This is the response of Amy Block Joy to your letter dated August 15, 2007. Below are my responses to each of your fifteen allegations.

Allegation #1 (dean's office letter): "[Vicki] said you immediately became very angry, rose up out of your chair ..."

ABJ response to #1: I am not sure why [Vicki] has suggested that I was angry. I was surprised when [Vicki] burst into my office. I would describe my demeanor as busy, cordial and polite. My attached timeline (Exhibit 1) shows that I'd been very busy working on a document for the USDA that needed approval from the dean's office.

My memories of the dean's office's August 13th interrogation were still raw. As I began to fill in each of my separate responses, I discovered that their letter didn't include the responses I gave during that meeting. There was no mention of the date of the alleged incident nor of the emails I'd sent.

Since I was told by the vice-chancellor's office that the dean's office had been in communication with them, I assumed that the powerful Dean Lorenzo had been given the go-ahead. This approval would have been granted by someone at the top of the university, who always would have campus counsel involved.

My view of the university suddenly changed. I'd been honored to be a University of California faculty member all these years. But now, I felt differently. Wasn't the dean's office supposed to represent the high standards of the university?

I wondered, *What happened to due process? What on earth was going on in the* dean's office?

On Monday, August 20, I arrived at work early. I sent the dean's office a request for using eight hours of my vacation leave for Wednesday, August 29th.

When I was moved to the dean's office in January 2007, the terms of my university employment changed. Unlike any other academic, I was required to get advance written approval to use vacation and sick leave. This demand was a result of having blown the whistle on the fraud. However, I didn't think protesting at that time would be in my best interest. I decided that I'd suck it up and fully cooperate with all their rules.

Their request form required a written reason. I toyed around with all sorts of ideas. My initial desire was to tell them that I was meeting with my bulldog attorney! But caution won out and I considered other reasons for my vacation request: *Confidential; None of Your Business; Goofing Off.* I selected a more professional response: Personal.

I emailed my vacation request to Lorenzo and copied Percy, then waited an hour for a reply. As expected, they didn't respond.

I sent a second email requesting an extension of time to respond to the letter. I sent my request to Lorenzo and copied Percy. This time I also copied the vice-chancellor:

> Dear [Visiting Dean Lorenzo Maestro]:
>
> I am requesting an extension of time to September 7, 2007, for my written response to your August 15th letter.
>
> Sincerely, Amy Block Joy
>
> Cc: [Dean Percy Grossman]
> [Vice-Chancellor, Franklin Taylor-Starr]

Sure enough, Lorenzo replied immediately, okaying my proposed new date. He also copied the vice-chancellor and Dean Percy Grossman—and added a few more folks: Shirley Handover and Roland Babu.

From Monday, August 20, to Friday, I spent time every evening after work on my response. The following Monday, August 27, I emailed my draft to Michael Hirst in preparation for our Wednesday meeting.

My single-space four-page response was very colorful and dotted with facts. I included seven exhibits to provide documentation to most of my red-font responses. I was personally satisfied with what I'd written. My factual accounting of what happened, however, did sound a bit like a scholarly research article.

After I emailed my draft response, I faxed twenty additional pages from my home machine: the eight-page letter from the dean's office; my four-page timeline; and my documentation (exhibits 1 to 7).

August 29, 2007

Early on August 29th, I drove up to Sacramento. I arrived at Michael's office a few minutes before 9:30, entered his office, and introduced myself to his office manager. Michael came out of his office when he heard my voice. Tall, athletic and good-looking, he was wearing a suit.

"Good morning, Amy. Happy to see you," he said as we shook hands. He seemed genuinely concerned about my welfare.

Michael then took me to his conference room and said he wanted me to meet some of his team. He came back and introduced me, first to Brooke, another attorney, and then to Zachary, his forensic investigator.

"We've all read your draft response," he began, "and are impressed with your documentation."

We spent the first thirty minutes discussing my whistleblower case. Reviewing the Justice Department's indictment of Beverly Benford from March 2007, Michael indicated that the fact that the fraud I blew the whistle on was substantiated was important. Although the law doesn't state that the whistleblower's report must be substantiated to allege retaliation, it certainly supplied a claim with credibility.

We then discussed my retaliation complaint. I used my timeline to organize all the evidence. I had emails, faxes, and witness interviews.

We went over the documentation that I'd collected and discussed each item in detail. Michael asked me questions about the evidence that I'd collected and my recollections of all the activities that took place at Davis after I exposed the criminal activity.

"Michael," I said at the end of our hourlong discussion. "I want to keep my job. Is this possible?"

"Often an employer wants the employee who blew the whistle to leave as part of a settlement," he said. "But since it's important to you to keep the job, we will do everything we can to make that happen."

I saw Zachary nod in agreement.

———

A few days later, Michael emailed me the letter I would send under my signature. It was magnificent! Finally, someone was actually fighting for me!

> September 5, 2007
>
> [Lorenzo Maestro, Visiting Academic Dean]
> [Percy Grossman, Associate Dean]
>
> Dear [Academic Dean Maestro],
>
> Pursuant to your request, this responds to your letter of August 15, 2007, in which you sought to summarize our meeting of August 13, 2007.
>
> Before I can address the issues raised in your letter, we should honestly consider the context in which the meeting took place and, in a larger sense, the deterioration that I have experienced in my work environment since becoming a whistleblower.

As you know, I filed a whistleblower complaint to report fraud perpetuated through
the misuse of ... Program funds, adminis-
tered by the Department of [Food, Health,
and Society] in the College [of Innovations]
at UC Davis. Based on my whistleblower
complaint ...employee Beverly Benford has
been indicted by the U.S. Attorney's Office
and faces criminal trial later this year. And, as
reported in the headline of the *Sacramento Bee*
(3/16/07), the '[i]ndictment raises questions
about [the] program's oversight ... amid allegations that a campus department may have
benefited improperly from large amounts of
federal funds she handled.'

I believed it was my duty to report fraudulent, illegal conduct of which I became aware,
even if the conduct involved my employer
and presented the University in a bad light.
I still believe that I was correct in doing so.
Unfortunately, however, since filing the whistleblower complaint, I have been subjected to
continuing harassment and unfair treatment
at work. It has become apparent that my supervisors and colleagues resent my having
blown the whistle—resent my having done
the right thing—and wish to punish me for
it. Sadly, your letter continues that trend.

Michael was a gifted writer. The clarity of his statements
regarding my doing the right thing and his pointing out
the response of my supervisors and colleagues was hugely
satisfying!

> Concerning the issues you raise, once again, in trying to do the right thing, I observed and responded to inappropriate conduct on the part of [an] ... employee, [Vicki Skipper], who advised another employee, [Rebecca Fukumoto], to falsify her time records. While others at the University may believe that falsifying time records is acceptable, I do not. I told [Ms. Skipper] so and cautioned her about it. Weeks later, in her exit interview, without ever having said so before, she accused me of allegedly threatening and shouting at her during a meeting ... several weeks previously. Apparently you have chosen to credit her accusations.

Michael got right to the point: Vicki's advising Rebecca to use overtime to increase her salary was essentially telling Rebecca to falsify time records.

> But even a cursory investigation of the facts surrounding the incidents discussed in your letter would have revealed that the allegations are entirely without merit. Perhaps you already know this. But if you were truly interested in determining the validity of those accusations, you would have interviewed others who could confirm or refute them. This seems so elementary that I am troubled by your failure to do so.

> Particularly troubling to me is your unwillingness to speak to the material witnesses I suggested during our meeting on August 13, 2007. Did you also choose to believe unfounded and refutable allegations ... to add credibility to [Vicki Skipper's] story? ... Did

you think that including unsubstantiated and never reported verbal abuse from ... [county colleagues] would strengthen your letter? As such, I am left with the impression that you do not really care about the facts, but instead wish to continue the unfair and unwarranted retaliation against me for having reported fraud at the University.

The next page of the letter provided my witness accounts in a series of exhibits, including Rebecca's email confirmation about the inappropriate advice by Vicki on July 18, my email discussion on July 23rd with Vicki regarding her breach of policy, Vicki's correction to Rebecca on July 23, and the testimony of my staff that they were not interviewed by anyone from the dean's office.

The facts, as I have told you, are that during lunch on Wednesday, July 18, 2007, [Vicki] recommended that [Rebecca] increase her compensation by falsifying her overtime hours. Had you spoken to [Rebecca], you would have confirmed that this conversation took place. Because you have not done so, I have attached an email from [Rebecca] quoting her recollection of the conversation ([Rebecca] 8/21/07, attached as Exhibit 1). She recalls that [Vicki] stated: "OK, now, [Roland] will probably kill me for saying this but what I think you should do is figure out what the analyst position would make and record that in OT hours." As [Rebecca] reports, that statement "took me a bit by surprise," because the suggestion was "counter to what I would have expected from someone at that level."

Following the inappropriate comments to [Rebecca], I met with [Vicki] to caution her on July 23rd and wrote to formalize our conversation immediately following the discussion (Block Joy 7/23/07 email, attached as Exhibit 2). I advised [Vicki] that her conduct "does not adhere to University policy." I stated that "we have discussed the issue. You said you would [email Rebecca] and correct the mistake. I agreed that this would be sufficient."

[Vicki] confirmed her statements to [Rebecca] by email that same afternoon ([Vicki Skipper] 7/23/01 email, attached as Exhibit 3) ...

[Vicki]'s inappropriate comments were not the subject of the brief meeting she had with me on 7/20/07, the meeting in which she claims I threatened her ... As you probably already know, and certainly would if you had conducted any investigation, my demeanor during ... July 20th was entirely appropriate and professional.

Indeed, Ginny Buckner was in her office next door during my meeting with [Vicki]. Again, though I asked you to confer with Ms. Buckner about the meeting, you have chosen not to do so. Accordingly, I attach an email of her observations (Buckner 8/14/07 email, attached as Exhibit 4). She states:

"This is in response to your question ... late afternoon of July 20th ... I absolutely would have noticed voices being raised in your office and this was not the case ..."

Clearly, though you have chosen simply to believe [Vicki]'s story, the evidence shows that the story is false.

While thankfully, the facts of the incident are verifiable, many of my personal interactions with you and [Dean Grossman] are not. I cannot express to you how disappointed and personally hurt I am by your conduct towards me. You have demonstrated again and again, that my decision to blow the whistle and report wrongdoing will not be forgiven or forgotten by my superiors. As such, you have continued to make my experience at work intolerable. I had hoped that you would protect me from malicious gossip and unfair accusations. Instead, you have contributed to the effort to discredit me and make my work life as unpleasant as possible. I believe that you understand what I am saying and recognize the pain that your actions are causing me.

I should not have to undergo this treatment from you or others ...

Michael included a page of legal citations, including the UC whistleblower protection policy from 2002; the California Labor Code; the Ninth Circuit statement on the statute, and a case law example from the California Supreme Court. He had done brilliant work for me, for which I will always be grateful.

The conclusion of the letter hit the bull's-eye like a shot of self-esteem!

> Simply put, I cannot continue to work under the unfair treatment I have experienced from you and others. Under the law and University policy, I should not have to. As my supervisor, I am asking you for your help and understanding. Accordingly, please advise me within 30 days what steps you intend to take to improve my work conditions and allow me to perform my job free of harassment and retaliation.
>
> Sincerely,
> Amy Block Joy

I reread the letter as I printed copies for Lorenzo, Percy, and Vice-Chancellor Taylor-Starr.

September 5, 2007

On Thursday, September 5, at 4:33 p.m., I hand-delivered my response in a plain white envelope. I gave copies to the administrative assistants of Lorenzo, Percy, and the vice-chancellor.

That very day, I received the university's response to my request for improved work conditions. The university hired a private fact-finder to investigate my retaliation claim.

Vice-Chancellor Taylor-Starr sent me an email notifying me that an "impartial, non-University party" had been hired to review both my retaliation complaint and Vicki's alleged incident of workplace violence.

I breathed a sigh of relief. Now that the university was put on notice, I expected that I'd be left alone to do my work in peace.

I was so wrong.

4 | Investigator Cruz

September 6, 2007

I arrived at my office early the next morning. In August, I'd planned a staff party to celebrate our success with getting the program back on track. None of my staff knew about the letter from the dean's office or that there was another investigation brewing. I didn't want them to worry that my future at the university, and probably theirs, was in jeopardy.

In fact, nobody even knew that I'd contacted an attorney. I didn't tell anyone, not my family or my friends, about the letter or my meeting with Michael.

I brought strawberries and homemade lemon scones for the meeting. We gobbled them up with some coffee while humming our new theme song: "Where Is the Love?"

We giggled at our silly joke. Initially, when Beverly was indicted by the U.S. Attorney in March 2007 and it was a front page story in the newspaper, a lot of the people that we'd worked with for years abruptly stopped coming by to visit. Many of them had been close friends of Beverly, so their apparent love for the soon-to-be-sentenced-employee disappeared quickly.

After the party, I returned to my office to get the ball rolling for the program's October 1 start date. I drafted an announcement to spread the good news. Then I completed a spreadsheet of names, addresses, and funding totals for each of my colleagues. Using Rebecca's calculations to finalize the spreadsheet, I emailed the document to the UC Davis accounting office. Of the sixty-five names on the list, twenty-one were colleagues who'd tried to get me fired!

I was grateful that Michael had prepared a powerful reply to the dean's office. *Those deans should think twice before calling me over for another interrogation,* I told myself. It was a great relief to get back to the job I was paid to do.

Looking out of my first floor office window, I watched a baby horse running in circles. The foal was prancing happily while his proud parents looked on. The Department of Food, Health, and Society was on the edge of the campus, with the university stables across the street. It was a quiet and serene place to work.

It felt like a regular workday. No longer upset by the petty inconveniences of people ignoring my phone calls and emails, I wasn't going to be disturbed by those who shunned me at meetings. I was happy that I'd taken the high road.

My program was about to embark on a new path and my first step would be a statewide conference to bring everyone together for training and networking. This was my administrative plan for getting folks back to work and ending the gossip that seemed to have a life of its own.

The foal, walking side-by-side with his cream-speckled mother, was on his way to the trough when my phone rang.

"Hello, this is Amy Block Joy," I said answering the telephone.

"Hello, Dr. Joy, my name is Isabelle Cruz," said a woman with an earnest voice. "I've been hired by the university to investigate your retaliation complaint. I'm calling to set up an appointment to meet with you."

"Thank you for getting in touch with me," I answered, surprised that she'd called so quickly. My complaint letter was only twelve hours old!

Investigator Cruz gave me a brief sketch of the investigative process and said that I'd be interviewed first.

"I have a list of people whom I'll be interviewing," she said, and added that a high-level faculty member from another campus would be on her team. I'd meet that person later.

"We're going to do a fact-finding investigation based on the issues presented in your letter," she told me briefly. I'd been heavily involved in a number of fact-finding investigations over the past year, so I was well-versed in the interview process.

"When would you like to meet?" I asked.

"The sooner the better. I have time on Monday, September 10. Does that day work for you?"

"Yes," I answered. "What's a good time?"

"How about 9:00 to 9:30 a.m.?"

"Nine a.m. is fine," I said slowly. "Investigator Cruz," I added, "I think we're going to need a couple of hours."

"In that case, let's start at 8:45. I'll come to your office on the Davis campus," she said.

"I'll email you directions," I suggested. She gave me her email address.

After we hung up I searched the Internet to read about her background. Isabelle Cruz had an impressive résumé. She was an employment investigator with a special focus on workplace harassment and one of the partners in a Sacramento firm of five. I noted that she'd done a stint in the general counsel's office at UC San Diego, which meant that she'd be familiar with the university policies and procedures.

It didn't matter what side of the university fence she came from, my evidence was solid. I emailed her directions to my office with some introductory information:

1. In August 2006, I blew the whistle on fraud and embezzlement at UC Davis. My allegations of fraud were substantiated.

2. I'd caught Beverly Benford, my program coordinator, using federal funds for personal benefit. According to the Justice Department's news release in March 2007 on her indictment, she'd stolen about $160,000 in electronic goods and travel reimbursements.

3. The case became complex almost immediately, with other persons benefiting from or involved in Benford's theft.

4. The minute I blew the whistle in August 2006, I was subjected to retaliation.

5. Retaliatory activities increased when Beverly's indictment was reported in the media in March 2007, and intensified in July 2007 following the release of the investigatory findings by internal audit.

I wanted to add that I expected the university to protect me from retaliation and that I was surprised that retaliation was still occurring twelve months later. In fact, I suspected that the release of the investigatory findings to dean's office was a motivating factor in the retaliation. I'd reviewed the findings on July 3, 2007. The report documented that I was intentionally excluded from communications between Benford and the departmental chair regarding $500,000 in purchases that benefited the department, including two departmental servers, conference room video equipment, renovations, and salary charges for Raymond's research.

These unapproved expenditures weren't detected by the university, and I believed they had been approved by someone in the dean's office. Was Dean Percy Grossman the one who authorized these purchases? He was in charge of my program. I suspected that he knew what was going on and the retaliation was meant to silence me.

But speculations weren't facts, so I left them out of my email.

> 6. On September 5, 2007, I filed a complaint alleging that my supervisor [Dean Percy Grossman] and his counterpart, [Academic Dean Lorenzo Maestro], engaged in retaliation against me for blowing the whistle on fraud at the university. They didn't protect my reputation and I believe participated in a smear campaign to discredit me.

I wrote a final sentence, "Their actions constituted whistleblower retaliation and it's against the law," and hit the send button.

Hearing the email whooshing away, I felt empowered and ready to speak with Investigator Cruz.

Before leaving my office that evening, I double-checked that the university hadn't changed its whistleblower protection policy, dated October 4, 2002. I was concerned that somewhere in the Legal Department, the general council was gearing up to replace its outdated anti-retaliation policy.

When I blew the whistle in 2006, I'd signed and dated an online form. My signature was to certify that I was telling the truth. I wondered how many cases were thrown out because the whistleblower didn't sign that obscure one-page form, modestly entitled "Form B."

Putting a date on Form B was also relevant. Having been a whistleblower for twelve months, I knew that the "retaliation" clock starts ticking the minute you blow the whistle. Cases have been thrown out for just missing one of many complex filing requirements.

I'd asked many university officials for examples of retaliation. Instead of providing them, the official in charge of whistleblower cases always promptly sent me the 2002 university policy:

> The University of California is committed to protecting employees … from … retaliation for having made a protected disclosure …

The ten-page document was stuffed full of intriguing concepts and technical definitions:

> **Improper Governmental Activity:** "Any activity undertaken by the University or an employee … and … is in violation of any state or federal law or regulation, including … corruption, malfeasance, bribery, theft, … fraudulent claims, fraud, coercion, conversion, malicious prosecution … or willful omission to perform duty …"

> **Protected Disclosure:** "Any good faith communication that discloses or demonstrates an intention to disclose information that may evidence either … improper governmental activity …"

> **Retaliation Complaint:** "Any written complaint by an employee … which alleges retaliation for having made a protected disclosure … together with a sworn statement, made under

penalty of perjury, that the contents of the complaint are true or are believed by the complainant to be true."

Procedures for filing a complaint were complex. There were tons of people, offices, and places to go to file a complaint, including supervisors, department chair, the director of Human Resources, the LDO, the vice-provost of Academic Relations, and the chancellor.

I'd already consulted with every one of the people on the list, save the chancellor!

> In order for a retaliation complaint to be accepted, the complainant must allege that:
>
> a) he or she filed a report ... alleging improper governmental activities ...
>
> b) he or she was threatened, coerced, commanded, or prevented by intimidation ...

And finally, the evidence needed to prove retaliation was explained on pages 6 through 9:

> California Government Code Section 845. 10(e) ... a retaliation complaint ... that once the complainant demonstrates by a preponderance of the evidence that he or she engaged in activity protected by the University's Whistleblower Policy and that such activity was a contributing factor in the alleged retaliation, the burden of proof shall be on the ... University to demonstrate by clear and convincing evidence that the alleged retaliatory action would have occurred independent of

the employee's engagement in a protected disclosure.

In other words, I would have to *demonstrate with evidence* that Percy and Lorenzo treated me one way before I blew the whistle and another less favorable way afterwards.

A Google search on *retaliation* wasn't helpful. Research was slim. I found articles about cases being tossed due to technicalities: missing an obscure deadline or having sent the complaint to the wrong person. I was unable to locate any substantiated retaliation complaints, probably because they were sealed and not available for public inspection.

Retaliation was an expected result of whistleblowing and the spectrum of adverse actions was broad. Being fired, demoted, or transferred to an undesirable location were typical responses. However, I found cases of more extreme action against the whistleblower, including reputation damage, career demolition, and blacklisting.

After reading a number of chilling accounts of tragedy and financial ruin, I decided that I wasn't about to become one of those whistleblower statistics!

September 10, 2007

On Monday, September 10th, Investigator Cruz arrived in my office promptly at 8:45 a.m. She introduced herself with a friendly outstretched hand.

Ms. Cruz was wearing an elegant linen suit which contrasted nicely with her auburn hair tied up in a French braid. Slim, athletic, and posed, she appeared engaging and businesslike. She had a slight musical accent but I wasn't sure if she was from the east coast or Latin America. From her extensive résumé, I guessed her age to be around forty but she could have easily have been in her early thirties.

"I've arranged for us to meet in the conference room across the hall," I told her. "That wall is made of glass," I said, pointing to the Venetian blinds that covered my wall, "and my staff would be able to hear our conversation."

"Glass?" she said, looking quizzical.

"Beverly Benford," I began, "designed my office and erected a glass wall between my desk and hers," I said. "I was alarmed by her strange decision. Beverly told me that the chair of the department, Raymond Savage, had insisted on creating this academic crypt," I added, half-joking.

I picked up my retaliation investigation file box and we moved next door to the conference room. Even at 8:45 the room was chilly from the air conditioning blasting cold air above us.

"Do you have a copy of my whistleblower report?" I asked.

"Yes," she answered, pointing to her large leather brief-case. "I've read your report and was given a copy of the in-vestigative results from internal auditing," she added, sitting down across from me.

I sat at the corner of the beautiful maple table and turned my chair so I could face Ms. Cruz. The size of the table made it difficult to sit across from her. I glanced around at the lush video-electronic equipment, added in 2005 to the tune of $11,500. This equipment purchase had been initiated by Beverly and approved by Raymond behind my back. Some-one in the dean's office must have authorized this high-end purchase but because I wasn't privy to the paperwork, I'd no idea who signed off on it.

"I want to hear from you directly," she began "about what happened. Do you want to start by telling me about your work?"

Used to providing a short introduction to my twenty-seven years of service at the university, I covered my faculty appointment and my work as the director of a $14 million program for food stamp clients in one minute.

"I'm sure you already know that my former program co-ordinator Beverly Benford has been indicted by the U.S. At-torney," I said at the end of my brief introduction.

"Thanks for that background," she said. "Now, do you want to tell me in your own words about your retaliation complaint?"

I nodded. Holding my September 5th letter in my hand, I leaned toward the investigator. This was the first time that I was allowed to speak to someone at the university about what happened *to me*.

"Before I begin," I said to her, "I should introduce you to the various individuals that I will be discussing."

I went over each of them one by one.

"First, there's Beverly Benford, my former program co-ordinator and the embezzler. She was put on investigatory leave a year ago and resigned on October 31, 2006. And ..." I paused a little, "there's Raymond Savage, the former chair of the department and the person who approved and signed her fabricated travel reimbursements and inappropriate pur-chases."

I decided that it wasn't necessary for me to tell her that he also used the federal funds intended for poor families to fund his own basic laboratory research. It was already in the audit report.

"I'm the director of the nutrition program, ..." I began, and managed to stop myself before adding *where the funds were stolen*. I finished the sentence with "...that you've read about in those investigative reports. I have continued to di-rect this program and have received preliminary approval for $13 million for next fiscal year."

I wanted the fact that our budget had been approved to sink in. This verifiable finding was relevant to my complaint. Timing was everything!

"There's Dean Percival Grossman," I added. "Percy is the associate dean in charge of the program and currently my supervisor." I left off the part about his being a former friend and ally.

"After the fraud was uncovered, I was moved to the Dean's office," I said slowly. "This was in January 2007," I continued. "When I'd go over there to meet with Dean Grossman, my new supervisor, I tried to talk to him about program needs, but instead he asked me personal questions about my emotional health," I told her.

"Personal questions? ..." she probed.

"Every time he'd call me over to his office, he quizzed me about therapy. I told him repeatedly that I wasn't in therapy and I wasn't taking medication. He told me that people were sending him confidential information. I felt he was trying to intimidate me," I said.

I looked at the investigator. "I found his questions to be disturbing, but I didn't want to rock the boat," I added, then stopped.

"You don't need to be concerned about anything you tell me," Ms. Cruz stated. "It's OK to tell me everything, even if you're not sure if it's relevant," she added. "The purpose of the investigation is to sort out exactly what happened."

"OK," I said. "I've known Percy for decades. His attitude about me changed. *Before* I blew the whistle, he gave me the impression that he admired *my work*," I said. "After I blew the whistle, he was ... ahh ... different. He told me to get therapy! He never said things like this before I became a whistleblower."

"Was this the first time you experienced this change in his attitude toward you?" she asked.

"There's been previous unfair treatment over the past six months," I said. "Percy received a letter signed by twenty-one of my colleagues. This was essentially a petition to remove me from office."

I pulled out the petition from the files that I'd brought with me. "Things got stirred up right after I was moved to the dean's office in January. My colleagues starting giving me the silent treatment," I said, and handed her a copy of the letter.

"The petition was addressed to Dean Percy Grossman," I pointed to the first page which had a handwritten note from Percy. "I think it was supposed to be a secret, but I was tipped off by a friend, and I immediately requested a copy. Percy faxed it to me on March 2, 2007," I told her, "from his home in Berkeley."

Investigator Cruz glanced at the petition quickly and put it down next to her notebook.

"I had the feeling that people were saying negative things about me," I said. "I tried to ignore all of it because I didn't want it to affect my productivity. Previous interactions over the last nine months with the dean's office have led me to believe that they aren't protecting my reputation. They haven't allowed me to respond to the issues raised."

"What kind of issues?" Investigator Cruz asked.

"Frankly, there seems to be a lot of gossip and rumors. I don't know what people were actually saying," I hesitated wondering if she'd get the picture, "but, people were avoiding me like the plague."

She kept writing.

"It was both distressing and perplexing," I added. I could hear my voice growing stronger as I added the following pattern that I'd observed over time.

"I exposed criminal activity," I continued, "and that created a lot of anger and misinformation. I'm bummed that my colleagues are still avoiding me. The investigation is winding down. Their angst should also be winding down too!" I told her. "It's been a year. Least we not forget, it was Beverly who committed the fraud!"

I carefully avoided blurting out the c-words: *collusion, conspiracy, corruption,* and *cover-up.* "Things should be settling down now—however, apparently, I'm the one who embarrassed the university!"

"It feels like the dean's office wants me to go," I said with a whisper. "If I'm no longer at Davis then the whole fraud problem might just …" I snapped my fingers, "disappear."

Ms. Cruz flipped the page in her note book. I looked down at my typed list of names.

"And there's just a couple more people …" I said aiming to be polite and discreet. "The other folks from the dean's office include Academic Dean Lorenzo Maestro, and Shirley Handover, the Human Resources director for the college," I said and watched her write down the names.

"I really don't know Dean Maestro. His role is still a mystery," I added. "However, when he accused me of violence in the workplace without having made any attempts to look into the facts or even talk to witnesses," I said clearly, "I was concerned about due process."

"I consider both his actions and inactions to be retaliatory," I stated. "I have no idea if Shirley Handover was involved or not."

I checked off the names that I'd already discussed on my list.

"Another person is my former supervisor, Professor Fred Stone," I began. "He was the vice-chair during my attempts to resolve the issue internally," I added. "Fred became chair just before I blew the whistle, and later he was asked to step down as the departmental chair. Dr. Stone was hugely impacted by the fraud investigation."

I gave Ms. Cruz a copy of the email that Fred had distributed widely on March 21, 2007, where he reported that he was asked to step down by the Dean's office.

"Fred and Percy both told me that there were numerous complaints filed against me," I said. "I asked the Provost's office if there were any outstanding negative issues in my personnel file. I was told unequivocally no."

I waited for Ms. Cruz to catch up.

"My current staff members are very dedicated and have been working very hard with me to keep the program afloat," I told her. "Their names are Ginny, Rebecca, and Ryan," I said, indicating that they'd all supported me.

"A former staff member, Terrence…ahh…left in January 2007. He wasn't a happy camper!" For some reason, I couldn't even remember Terrence's last name!

"And then there's Vicki," I said. "Vicki is the person at the heart of my complaint," I declared with some urgency. "Vicki was hired by the dean's office in July to help me. I'd been under the gun for months, so, it was a big relief to have someone to help out! But that's not what happened."

Shaking my head in disbelief, I continued.

"When Vicki arrived in July, my program had received interim approval. Vicki entered the scene right after we'd completed all the work for restoring our future!"

I wasn't sure if I should include my speculations. I'd done so when I was interviewed by the police and internal auditing about my initial embezzlement discovery in March 2006 and the discussion I'd had with Beverly and Raymond. But this interview was different—this was about my future!

"I'm going to speculate now," I said deciding to go for it. "Percy, my supervisor, was the head honcho responsible for the program. In early July, I, and the dean's office, received a draft audit report. There was evidence that the embezzlement and misappropriation was accomplished without my knowledge or approval. There were also budgetary manipulations that were not detected by the university. The total was about $500,000!"

Investigator Cruz was writing rapidly and flipping pages to keep up.

"In other words, the dean's office messed up big time! And I think," I said, waiting for Ms. Cruz to look up at me, "the retaliation was meant to keep me quiet!"

She said nothing and returned to writing on her notepad.

"I think now would be a good time to tell you about the meeting on August 13, in the dean's office."

I got up to look out the small beveled-glass window on the conference room door to see if anyone was seated outside the room. The Do Not Disturb sign on the door clanged when I checked to make sure the door was tightly closed.

As I began to talk, the sound of her pencil scribbling on the yellow tablet faded away. No longer shivering from air conditioning, I found relief in telling her what happened.

It took thirty minutes to tell Ms. Cruz my recollection of the meeting on August 13 with Lorenzo, Percy, and Shirley. I went over the notes that I'd scribbled during the meeting. She asked very few questions during my monologue, although one stuck out as very relevant.

"You said that Dean Maestro told you six times that Vicki was highly regarded in the college and a person of high integrity. Did anyone during the meeting say anything about your integrity?"

"No. Nothing."

Investigator Cruz had taken extensive notes and wanted a copy of my scribblings from the August 13 meeting. My notes contained six checkmarks next to the phrase that Lorenzo kept repeating: "Vicki = highly regarded/high integrity."

She wrote down something about the six checkmarks on my notes. "Tell me more about Vicki," she said quietly.

"I connected with Vicki very quickly and was expecting to lean on her for advice. She had a lot of experience. At least that's what I was told by Shirley. More importantly, she had a good relationship with the dean's office, and she really bonded with Rebecca!"

"What happened between Vicki and Rebecca?" Inspector Cruz asked.

"On July 18th, Rebecca came to the office so that we could go over our final submission to the USDA. Vicki was impressed with Rebecca. After the training session, Vicki suggested that the group have lunch together. During the lunch, we talked about personal things, and I thought it was a social lunch."

I then told Ms. Cruz what I overheard Vicki telling Rebecca and showed her the email that Rebecca had written about the conversation. Rebecca stated that Vicki had told her, "Roland would probably kill me for saying this, but what I think you should do is put down overtime hours to get to the higher salary that you want."

"I got quiet and tried not to have my mouth drop open," I told Investigator Cruz.

Ms. Cruz then asked me point-blank if I ever yelled at Vicki. I adamantly denied it.

"Have you ever yelled at anyone?" she continued.

"No ... although with Beverly I did raise my voice," I said. "During a meeting Beverly got very angry and was yelling at me, and I did raise my voice when I asked her to leave my office," I admitted. "Everyone next door and in the hall could hear that exchange! I asked Beverly to return to her office and cool off," I explained.

"It's not uncommon for various folks to raise their voice at me," I said factually. "I make unpopular budget decisions and it goes with the territory. But yelling is not my style."

I then recounted the meeting I'd had with Vicki on July 23rd.

"I met with Vicki at 1 p.m. to discuss her advice to Rebecca regarding use of overtime. Vicki listened and appeared nonplussed. She admitted it was a mistake on her part, and said that she shouldn't have said that to Rebecca and that she'd correct her advice. I thought my meeting with her went very well. Vicki seemed OK. She was quiet, thoughtful. I thought Vicki handled it well. I sent a very lengthy email to Vicki with a copy to the dean's office at 1:42 p.m. to summarize the meeting."

I gave Investigator Cruz a copy of the email with the date and time highlighted.

"No one at the dean's office admitted to me that they'd seen this email," I told her, wondering if she'd had any insight into this omission.

"Thanks," she said taking the copy and putting it into her pile. "Let's go back to August 13: What happened after the meeting at the Dean's office?" she asked.

I looked at the clock in order to pace myself. It was already 10:30! Investigator Cruz must have noted my concern about time; she told me she didn't have another interview until after lunch.

I opened one of the bottles of water that I'd put in the room before the meeting, and poured some into a cup.

"Would you like some water?" She nodded, and I handed her a bottle and a cup.

"Right after the August 13 meeting, I went straight to my office," I began, "and tried to piece together the puzzle by creating a timeline."

"Here's a copy," I said handing my document to her. As she studied the first page, I told her how exactly I constructed it.

"I printed all the emails from my computer that I'd sent on July 20th, highlighted the time on the email, and included it on my timeline," I said taking another sip of water. "These emails provided a date stamp of my whereabouts."

I could hear her pencil scratching on the tablet.

"I also have other documentation for July 20th. I sent twenty-eight emails and one fax that afternoon. Each of those emails is listed by the time it was sent.

"I've recounted my entire relationship history with Vicki, starting on July 2 when I met her in Shirley's office until the meeting with Lorenzo, Percy, and Shirley on August 13th."

"How long did Vicki work?" she asked.

"Five days in total. Vicki began working at 1 p.m. on July 11th and she left on July 25th," I said. "She was out ill for several days," I said, pointing out the actual days on my time-line. "She did tell Ginny that she was leaving and sent an email to Rebecca," I said, and handed her a copy of the email Vicki sent to Rebecca on July 25th.

"What happened after Vicki's departure?" Ms. Cruz asked.

"I tried to find a copy of her resignation letter," I said. "I thought it was strange that nothing was communicated to me at all from Vicki or from anyone at the Dean's office. When I called the HR director and left a message that I'd like a copy of Vicki's resignation letter, she never returned my telephone call.

"My last communication with anyone regarding Vicki was when I signed her time record and took it over to the Dean's office," I said, handing her a copy of Vicki's leave record.

"I assumed that Vicki's new position meant that she just transferred over to another department and that all I needed to do was sign her time slip.

"I didn't hear anything about Vicki, her exit interview with the dean's office, or anything else about this until the August 13th meeting," I reported.

"During the meeting I was told that this issue would not be written up," I said, sighing. "On August 17th, I received a letter from the dean's office regarding their allegations against me," I added, pointing to the letter that I'd placed next to me on the table.

"At that point, their message seemed really clear," I said looking directly at Investigator Cruz and waiting for her to ask me.

She looked up from her notebook.

"What was their message?"

"They wanted me out," I stated, looking directly at her. She didn't flinch.

"You've provided a lot of details," she said as she closed her notebook. "Is there anything else you'd like to add?"

"I'm good," I said feeling energized. I gathered up my files and put them back in my file box.

"OK. Let's go back to your office and finish up," the investigator said, picking up her briefcase.

My office was located across the hall. I opened the door of the conference and then the door of my office. We both went inside.

"Where do you sit when you meet with someone?" she asked.

I sat down in my desk chair and swiveled around to face Ms. Cruz.

"Where did Vicki sit," she asked, "on July 23rd?"

I pointed to the chair by the wall of my office, about three feet away from my own chair. She put her briefcase on that chair.

"Talk out loud in your normal speaking voice," she said.

"What do you want me to talk about?" I asked.

"Anything you want to say to my briefcase," she answered.

Immediately, Polonius's advice to Laertes from *Hamlet* popped into my head, and I began talking to her briefcase: "'This above all: to thy own self be true, and it must follow, as the night the day, thou canst not then be false to any man.'"

She darted out of my office.

I felt a little funny speaking aloud to a briefcase in my empty office. But I continued as directed to repeat the quote a couple more times until she burst back into my office.

"Now I want you to shout and yell," she said handing me a book from my shelf. "Read this page in a loud, shouting voice."

She handed me the book, *Food Politics* by Marion Nestle, and I began to shout. I became self-conscious and felt my face flush:

"'DO CAMPAIGN CONTRIBUTIONS, TRIPS, AND PRESENTS BUY CORPORATE INFLUENCE OVER GOVENMENT DECISIONS? MUCH EVIDENCE SUGGESTS THAT THEY DO, AND IN PROPORTION TO THE AMOUNT SPENT ...'" I shouted with vigor as Ms. Cruz hurried out of my office.

My face must have turned bright red, but I continued to shout aloud until she burst back into my office and said I could stop reading.

She wrapped up by giving me a very professional response, which I took as a compliment: "You're very organized. Thank you for preparing the documentation. Could you send each of the emails you used in your timeline? I'd like to have the original electronic version."

I walked Investigator Cruz to her car, chit-chatting about my latest paper, which calculated a cost-benefit analysis of saved medical costs. I wanted her to know that the fraud, the investigations, and all the other stuff wasn't going to keep me from doing the best work possible for the program.

After I returned to my office, I was greeted by all my staff. They were bursting to tell me about the investigator coming in and out of the office next to mine.

"She was checking to see if she could hear you through the walls," Ginny said.

"Could she?" I asked.

"Everyone could hear you!" Ginny said giggling. "We had a hard time trying not to laugh when you began shouting about campaign contributions!"

"The first time she came in we were mystified who you were talking to," Ginny added grinning.

I flashed on her leather briefcase sitting in the chair.

"Of course, when you were repeating the phrase 'To thine ownself be true, and it must follow ...' we thought you must have some sort of dignitary in your office," Ginny added, winking at me.

"Oh, wow ... Sorry to disturb you."

"Thou canst not then be false to any man," Ginny answered, laughing.

5 | Attempts to Discredit Me

I returned to my office to thank Investigator Cruz via email: "Thank you for meeting with me today," my email began. "I'm forwarding the nine email exhibits we discussed in my timeline. You'll receive each one separately."

I was quite pleased with the interview and was confident that Ms. Cruz would do a fair and thorough investigation.

September 2007

The dean's office sent a second helper to provide assistance. This time they hired one of the authors of the OR, Glenda Quinn. Glenda, well known at Davis as an efficiency expert, was young and unflappable. I expected she'd be good at following orders from the powers that be at the dean's office.

Glenda held mini-meetings with my team. She avoided meeting with me. I made it a priority to attend her haphazardly scheduled meetings with the hope of winning her over. We were on the brink of moving forward, and I didn't want another Vicki-style dustup.

Meanwhile, I was working alone on a massive USDA final report, analyzing evaluation results from 120,000 families. With dozens of tables of food consumption data to examine, I needed analytically trained staff, so I asked Glenda to get the hiring ball rolling. Preliminary results produced a showcase of program successes that I planned to use to re-connect with my colleagues. I wanted to remind them of our purpose: to improve the health and well-being of California's poorest children, adults, and families.

Glenda ignored my request to discuss the evaluation re-sults with my team, and it didn't take long for me to discover what she was up to. I found a confidential document tucked away in my Staff Meeting Minutes folder. Dated September 12th, the document contained Glenda's meeting minutes. The last page in the folder listed an assortment of negative comments about me.

It seemed somewhat sloppy for an efficiency expert. I wondered whether her misstep was intended to tip me off about a new plan to discredit me. The page was prepared for Dean Percy Grossman and his gang; I was somewhat amused by what Glenda wrote.

Entitled "Observations about Amy," it contained a laun-dry list of Glenda's opinions, including:

Amy organizes chaos.

Amy has limited administrative skills to direct work.

Amy's efforts are scattered and defers to others.

Amy asked Ryan to review a purchase order.

Amy manually adds up curriculum orders.

Amy proofed the Nutrition Plan.

I do not think Amy will change her leadership style.

Amy's decisions are scattered.

Amy lacks decision-making skills.

I do not think anyone can mentor Amy.

My retaliation complaint was just five days old, but Glenda's secret notes provided more evidence that the dean's office wasn't going to let up.

I read her notes several times, searching for anything positive. There wasn't any reference to the fact that the USDA was about to grant me another $13 million. In fact, my research on documenting the cost-effectiveness of the program, my twenty-seven years of credibility, and my work in assisting low-income families apparently didn't earn any brownie points from Glenda. Was her secret report supposed to be constructive? If so, then she might have included me on the distribution list. I suspected that instead it was a dean's office ploy to create a record of my administrative failings.

I sent an email to Investigator Cruz. I wanted to bring Glenda Quinn's negative comments into the light. I assumed that Ms. Cruz would inform Glenda that her secret notes had been discovered.

My brief email to Investigator Cruz contained three examples. I didn't want to focus too much of my attention on this juvenile incident, as I wanted her to handle it.

Ms. Cruz replied immediately that Glenda was going to be interviewed and that she'd ask her about the notes. Apparently, Glenda was already on her radar!

I met with Glenda later in the week. During the meeting I asked her directly about my leadership style, hoping to get her to talk to me honestly about her opinions. She deflected my query with a new spin.

"Are you going to stay?" Glenda said with an awkward tilt to her head.

"Yes," I answered and then shut up.

Glenda then produced a long-winded story about how she'd once been given the task of laying off a whistleblower and had to escort him out of the building because of the way he was behaving. She appeared to be proud of this particular accomplishment.

"Interesting," I said after a long pause. I was skeptical, particularly about her whistleblower label.

"Haven't you had enough?" Glenda asked me.

"What do you mean?"

"This must be very painful," she said flatly. Her tone was less than sympathetic, and I decided not to encourage her to go down that road.

"Are you planning on continuing as director?" Glenda persisted.

"Yes, I'm planning on continuing as director. There's still a lot of work to do to get the program back on track."

She seemed baffled by my attitude, so I asked her my own question.

"My question for you: Are *you* ready to rock and roll?"

I watched her eyes roll as she got up from her chair. Glenda just didn't have a sense of humor!

The next week I was invited to a snazzy USDA meeting, and I invited Glenda to join me. I thought it would be in my best interest for her to meet my USDA colleagues. I expected that she'd be thrilled to make a splash with the federal folks. Her ho-hum response made it clear: she really didn't want to go, which gave me the idea that Glenda might just be in way over her head!

I managed to twist Glenda's arm regardless, by arranging to drive her to the Sacramento meeting. She had no excuse.

She'd agreed to meet me in the parking lot by her campus office at exactly 9:20 a.m. so I could drive her to the meeting, which started at 10:00. By 9:40 there was still sign of her. Glenda was a no-show! As I waited for her in my car, I sent an apologetic email to a USDA colleague to let her know that we'd be late.

I was reluctant to leave without Glenda. I worried that things might go south quickly. She might tell the dean's office that I ditched her and gone to the meeting alone. So I called her repeatedly on my BlackBerry until she finally answered. Glenda tried to make it look like that I'd gone to the wrong parking lot. By the time she got into my car it was already after 10:00.

En route, I cheerfully told Glenda that I'd already emailed the USDA that we'd be late. I could tell she was nervous. When she spilled her can of Diet Coke all over her summertime shorts, I felt sorry for her. USDA meetings were much more formal than UC Davis. Glenda must have felt totally out of her league.

We arrived into the meeting room about twenty minutes late. The person in charge of the meeting interrupted the discussion to welcome us, and I introduced Glenda to the group. I told the officials that she was a consultant from the dean's office and encouraged her to speak. Glenda was silent—nothing to say.

I'd hoped that Glenda would observe that the USDA folks treated me as a professional, with respect and dignity. Would Glenda emerge as an independent thinker who could form her own conclusions? In the end, my attempts to change the playing field completely struck out!

<hr />

On Wednesday, September 26, I received an email in the evening that my salary and benefits would be decreased by 25 percent on October 1—only four days away! An administrator in the department had written:

> As Director and steward of the federal funds, I unfortunately can no longer justify funding ... and as of October 1, 2007, funding will cease ...

I wasn't surprised when I saw Percy's name on the memo. As alarming as that email sounded, I also wasn't unduly dismayed: University policy requires advance notification of at least thirty days for a salary reduction. I forwarded the email to Investigator Cruz and expected that there'd be some sort of resolution.

The very next evening I heard from Percy. He wrote: "I want to reassure you that your salary situation is being resolved and you will receive your normal paycheck this month."

I received an official approval letter from the USDA stating that my program would continue and was approved for $13 million. The letter arrived the day after Percy's memo, and I was ecstatic! In fact, the approval letter didn't mention any further audits, sanctions, or probationary periods.

Early the next morning, I sent out a brief announcement about our renewed funding under my directorship: "Colleagues, It gives me great pleasure to announce that our FFY 08 Program has been approved! Last night I received a letter ... FFY 08 budget for $12,790,293 ..."

My email was distributed to hundreds of faculty, staff, colleagues, as well as the dean's office staff. I received several congratulatory responses from a number of folks whom I hoped would return to work with me. I assumed that their confidence in my leadership was restored. Suddenly the tide had turned!

October 2007

My second interview with Investigator Cruz was scheduled for October 2, 2007. At this interview, I met the faculty co-investigator, Dr. Troy Archer, a retired professor from UC Irvine. He was tall, dignified, and well known for his pioneering research on heart disease. In contrast to the first interview process, both Investigator Cruz and Dr. Archer had a list of questions to ask me. Their questions were more personal and left me perplexed about the scope of their investigation.

"We'd like to talk to you about your past working relationships here at Davis," Investigator Cruz told me.

I was determined not to bad-mouth anyone. Not only did I feel it would be morally wrong, I thought it would be counter-productive. My goal was to re-connect with these folks!

"How would you describe your relationship with Crystal?"

Crystal Benny was someone that I'd know since 1999, when she took over the reins of my work from the UC Office of the President. She was also a UC graduate, but our education timelines didn't overlap. From 1974 to 1979, I was in the Nutritional Sciences Department at Berkeley, getting my doctorate. Crystal completed her master's degree a decade after I'd finished at Berkeley and then went to another university to get her PhD before coming to UC Davis.

"Crystal and I began working together in 1999. She had ideas on what she wanted to do and I respected her desire to be independent," I said tactfully.

"We were both working with low-income families, and I believe we shared a similar view on the value of education to improve nutritional well-being," I finished.

Investigator Cruz was writing and Dr. Archer nodded for me to continue.

"We combined efforts for about a year or two," I added trying to stay positive.

"Recently, there's been some conflict between us," I admitted. I decided that this was the time to let them know about her relationship with fraudster Beverly Benford.

"What kind of conflict?" Investigator Cruz asked me with some curiosity.

"She hired a relative of Beverly Benford," I said frankly. "I tried to meet with her to discuss my concerns with her directly," I began. "She wouldn't even call me back or respond to my emails," I added, embarrassed.

"I found out about this in December 2005, just before I discovered the misuse of funds," I told them. "This was a red-flag warning that made me highly suspicious. I spoke to the chair of our department, Dr. Raymond Savage, about my concern regarding Crystal and Beverly. Raymond said the relative would be using a different last name and that no one would know that she was related to Beverly."

Investigator Cruz didn't seem at all surprised, so I assumed that Crystal had already been interviewed.

"I told Raymond that it was ridiculous to think that people wouldn't know. I was totally against it and told him so in a letter I sent to him on February 27, 2006."

"You have an amazing recall for details," Dr. Archer said.

"Well, I guess my recall of this letter is because I wrote it and a day or so later discovered the fraudulent purchase order, so this letter became part of the whistleblower investigation," I explained. "I'll forward you the letter I wrote to Departmental Chair Savage about my concern."

"In the end, Dr. Savage reminded me that this was Crystal's decision and not mine," I told them. "I couldn't argue with that. But I heard that Crystal found out I'd talked to Raymond and I heard that she and Beverly were, um ... good friends."

Investigator Cruz didn't bring up the issue about my recent salary snafu, and I didn't mention that Crystal had been copied on the email memo that tried to reduce my university salary. Was this the reason Crystal was interviewed?

We spent another thirty minutes talking about my other colleagues, including Darci Small, a colleague that I was really fond of.

"Let's just say that I thought Darci was a good friend," I told them. "I think I must have been wrong about that," I said with some degree of uncertainty.

"In April of this year, Darci announced that she no longer would be involved in the program as of October 1. She provided plenty of time for someone to replace her—so I respected her professionalism," I added, trying to be positive. "It did concern me that she didn't want to stick around.

"In addition, one of her staff resigned and circulated a negative letter about me," I continued. "His name is Felix," I said. "When Felix said that he didn't want to be part of a program that I was directing," I added, "it reminded me of the stuff that was written in my colleagues petition to remove me."

Investigator Cruz told Dr. Archer that she'd send him a copy of the petition letter. I agreed to send them both the letter from Felix. Investigator Cruz nodded for me to continue.

"Felix had been all too happy to receive program funds to pay for his salary and benefits *before* I blew the whistle," I told them. Suddenly, I recalled that Felix was now employed by Crystal! What a small world. I wondered if he was going to be interviewed.

"It's been very upsetting that people aren't talking to me or replying to my work-related emails," I said. "In fact, many are either canceling meetings and conference calls or just not showing up. The result is that they are avoiding me," I sighed.

"It's been hurtful, confusing, and exhausting," I told them. "For the past year, I'd tried to get along with everyone, not step on anyone's toes, and do the best job possible. The isolation and alienation are the most difficult. What this experience has taken from me is peace of mind.

"On a positive note," I added, "I did manage to get another year of funding for the program—almost $13 million for the new fiscal year," I said smiling. "So even under these difficult circumstances, something's working!

"Right now, I'm polishing our evaluation results to showcase our program successes for my statewide conference. I'm hoping to get these folks back to business!" I saw

Dr. Archer flash a smile. I wondered if they were concerned that the interview process might upset me.

"Thank you for meeting with us today," Ms. Cruz said. "Do you have anything you'd like to add?"

I asked about their investigative timeline. Dr. Archer said that their investigation might take a couple more months but they were aiming to have their report done quickly. Investigator Cruz told me that they had several more interviews with people who were currently out of the country.

Before the meeting ended, she asked me if I wanted to include anyone else in my retaliation complaint. I wondered if she thought I'd bring up the secret notes written by Glenda Quinn.

"No, I believe that the retaliators are Deans Grossman and Maestro," I said conclusively.

The very next day, October 3, I was asked to meet with Roland Babu and Glenda at 10:00 a.m. to talk about my response to the OR. As usual, Glenda was late. Roland and I went over the next year's budget.

After Glenda arrived, the meeting became tense. I believed that the issue under discussion was that the dean's office wanted me to wipe the slate clean and hire new replacement staff. Glenda even hinted that I wouldn't be allowed to hire new staff with the former staff still in the office. I told them that I wanted to consult with campus counsel about layoffs.

Roland suddenly began asking questions about the fraud investigation. Stunned, I suggested that he get the information directly from Internal Auditing. I wasn't trying to be difficult—I just didn't understand why he was asking for information that I didn't have. He pounded his fist on his desk and raised his voice, claiming I was withholding information.

Taken aback and frightened by such an extreme reaction, I stopped the meeting and requested a ten-minute break. My heart was racing and I wasn't feeling well. I asked Roland's permission to leave his office for a few minutes. He shook his head back and forth indicating both a no and his displeasure. Glenda began talking rapidly about future plans for our website. I could barely speak.

Eventually I recovered. Nothing more was said about the fraud investigation and the meeting wrapped up. I returned to my office. Did my mention of consulting campus counsel send Roland into a tizzy?

I emailed Investigator Cruz that I'd changed my mind about whom to include in my retaliation complaint. I said that I decided to include another person. I sent her a detailed report of the "Roland incident."

A few hours later I received a phone call from Roland. He apologized for not being sensitive to my situation. I accepted his apology and sent another email to Investigator Cruz to disregard my previous email.

Someone must have read Roland the riot act!

———••———

I reviewed past emails from Roland to see if I could find a clue. I found almost nothing from Roland via email. Like Shirley, he simply didn't reply to my email requests. In fact, what I did find was many friendly emails from Percy, some of which had been copied to Roland. As I read them, I noticed that they were sent just before everything fell apart:

> … Thanks for all the good work you are doing. I think you've done wonderfully amidst all the turmoil and stress in recent months.

It looks to me like things are moving as we
would like, and it is due to your good work.

Other emails from Percy conveyed his appreciation of my
work: "Wow! What great news! I had not expected this
would materialize so quickly ... Congratulations. Look forward to talking to you ... Wonderful ... I do believe you are
well poised for the future."

Even more revealing was an email sent to me after I thanked
him for his support: "Thanks for your kind thoughts ... I'm
delighted ... I've enjoyed every moment of our work together."

I wasn't imagining that the dean's office view of me
changed: Percy's appraisal of my good work was clearly in
the record. Only since my whistleblowing had his attitude
taken a major turn for the worse.

Investigator Cruz sent me an email on October 12th to let
me know that she'd met with Glenda and had discussed her
notes: "Hi Amy ... I interviewed [Glenda] earlier today. You
should know that I asked her about the notes ... She is probably going to speak to you about this."

I requested a face-to-face meeting with Glenda right
away and she came over to see me. Glenda talked incessantly
about ways to improve our website. She didn't mention anything about her secret notes to the Dean's office. She wasn't
able to look me in the eye, and the only time I was able to
speak was when she paused to take in some oxygen.

Eventually, Glenda announced that she had another
meeting to attend and stood up to go. I tried again. "Glenda,
I appreciate your working with my team," I said cheerfully.
"I was wondering if you had any advice for me, specifically."

I waited. She looked down at the ground. Her silence was deafening.

"You're an experienced financial manager," I continued, "any management suggestions?" I said trying hard to invite her to talk about her notes. I wasn't going to confront her directly. Going by what had happened when I confronted Vicki about her policy breach, I didn't expect that Glenda would take that well.

I was disappointed that she didn't say anything to me about her notes, but I let it go. I'd hoped to clear the air with her, and I'd even planned to tease her about improving her 007 skills. I wanted this to be a learning experience for both of us. Unfortunately, until she was able to speak her mind honestly, our working relationship was doomed.

In mid-October, I asked the university to investigate what was happening with my postal mail. I hadn't received any letters, my professional journals, or even junk advertisements and catalogues for several weeks. My campus mailbox, located on the third floor of the department, was empty.

The missing mail included a reimbursement check from the UC Accounting office for $1013.98 for out-of-pocket travel expenses. I'd put in for them in early September and had been waiting since then. According to records, the university had approved my claim and a check for that amount had been cut on September 18. When it didn't arrive, I emailed the dean's office and requested that the university issue a new check. The dean's office asked Roland Babu to investigate.

Instead of investigating my lost check, Roland left me a voicemail message suggesting that I talk to the IT guys in the Dean's office. After I returned his call to explain that the issue concerned my *postal* mail, he tried again. His second reply was another telephone message that he'd received confirmation from the mail division on campus that they had my correct mailing address. Was Roland missing the point on purpose?

November 2007

On Tuesday, November 6, the university briefed me and others on the now completed fraud audit. I became worried that the information would create more distress. Colleagues from the Food, Health, and Society Department and the college were advised that another media circus was about to ensue. The forty-page audit report, already requested by the *Sacramento Bee*, was very detailed, exposing the increased amount of fraud and those involved.

After my early morning briefing, I sent an email requesting that my identity as the whistleblower be included in the university's press release. I sent the email to the university's attorney with the following statement:

> Thank you for briefing me ... As you already know, I feel that I have been a victim of retaliation and I believe this will only increase ... I feel that my only protection is by being known as the whistleblower ... I give my full approval to the university to release my identity.

I'd decided when I blew the whistle in 2006 that this was the right thing to do. There was no reason for the identity of the whistleblower to be a distracting mystery—especially when it was readily available from earlier news reporting.

That same day, I left the Davis faculty parking lot and headed home just before 6:00 p.m. It was dark and the lot was empty. When I made the first left turn out of the lot, I heard a screeching sound and turned off the radio to hear better. A few minutes later, turning right onto the frontage road near the freeway entrance, my car felt unsteady. I initially thought that the road had numerous potholes. But when I got to the freeway and began to accelerate, my car began shaking violently. I immediately slowed down to twenty miles per hour, then to ten, and finally to just five miles per hour. The car was still shaking, so I pulled onto the shoulder of the freeway to avoid being hit by the fast traffic.

I saw an open gas station at the next exit up the road. Holding tightly onto the steering wheel to try to control the shaking, I moved my car slowly toward the light. Many cars honked at me for the three miles that I drove on the shoulder of the freeway, hoping to make it safely to the Pedrick exit. I pulled my seatbelt tighter. Suddenly I heard a loud noise, the sound of an explosion, and my car veered off the shoulder into the dirt.

Physically I was fine, but in the dark on that empty road, I was frightened. I called my emergency service. While waiting for the CSAA Road Service to arrive, I got out of my car and moved away from the freeway into the dark field. I wondered if I should walk to the gas station up the road.

Instead, I stayed with my car and called several persons at UC Davis and left messages. The Director of Internal Auditing called me back right away. As I began to tell him about the incident, the emergency service vehicle arrived.

The automobile emergency service came to change the tire. He took off the hub cap of the rear passenger tire and used a flashlight to show me that one of the lug nuts wasn't screwed on properly. After he removed it, he showed me the damage. He said that the lug nut wasn't holding the tire properly and this had caused my car to become unsteady and the tire to blow out. He removed what was left of the tire— metal fibers were sticking out and large chunks of it were missing.

He checked the wear on the tire. The tire had had plenty of tread. I'd had no difficulty driving to Davis that day—the car wasn't unsteady and there wasn't any shaking.

We walked down the shoulder a bit to pick up the other pieces of tread on the road. This wasn't just a flat tire.

The CSAA guy wrote a note on his card as a witness to the tire destruction. He told me that I was very lucky that I wasn't driving fast on the freeway.

I reported the incident to the UC Davis police. Photographs were taken of the tire and pieces of tread, the damaged hub cap, and the stripped lug nut. I was given a case number the next day.

I sent another email to Investigator Cruz to document the incident. I told her that my car had been vandalized right after the negative attention surfaced from the first news story published by the *Sacramento Bee*.

By mid-November, I still hadn't received my reimbursement check, so I sent an email to Investigator Cruz on November 14th. I explained that my postal mail was being disrupted and expressed my disappointment in the dean's office's lack of response.

An investigator from the Provost's office mailed me a letter with *Confidential* stamped prominently on the outside next to their office address. He was checking to see when I received the letter. It never arrived. I notified Investigator Cruz about my concern over the missing reimbursement check.

Then, like magic, the missing September 18th check arrived! The envelope, which was clearly marked as a travel reimbursement check, looked like it'd been through the ringer. I speculated that someone had been holding it to frustrate me.

A few days later, I walked into the mailroom on the third floor. Walking in, I noted that people were standing around chatting—then suddenly the room emptied. I found an obscene picture hanging above my mailbox name. Someone had placed a picture and taped it over my box so that my name appeared under it, like a title.

I removed the picture and found three letters in my mailbox. Two of the three were confidential letters that had been ripped opened and then taped shut. On one of the envelopes someone had written "no longer here." On another, someone had drawn an "unhappy face."

In the wake of this, I insisted that the university mail division create a new mail stop on the first floor of the building, where my office was located. The mail division had no problem with the change in address. This freed me from further encounters with the folks upstairs.

Later that morning, my conference planning committee was meeting via conference call. Claudia Walker, my co-chair to plan the event, led the discussion. This was our fifth planning meeting.

Our committee included eight persons, two colleagues and six staff members. Glenda was supposed to be on the committee, but she was way too busy to participate. I even wondered if she planned to attend the event—she'd been canceling meetings with the committee after the release of the audit findings.

Claudia began the meeting with a discussion of the selection of our conference theme. The event, scheduled for

December 3rd and 4th, was something that I'd hope would offer me a new beginning.

Ginny reported the number of people who'd already registered for the conference. So far, we had a head count of a hundred and ten, with an expectation of about a hundred and fifty persons over the two-day event. All of the early-bird registrants were spending the night at the hotel. Our conference facility was a hotel next to the San Francisco Airport. My program paid all expenses, including meals, hotel, and transportation.

"Let's have an update on the 'show-and-tell' session," Claudia asked committee member Jonnie Tao. Jonnie had done an excellent job of organizing a poster session for the first afternoon of the event.

After Jonnie reported that fifteen persons had already sent in abstracts for their posters, another committee member reported on her work in organizing physical activity breaks throughout each day. We even planned to offer an early morning yoga session in one of the hotel rooms for anyone interested.

"I have some good news," Claudia reported halfway through the agenda. Our keynote speaker had agreed to conduct his interactive Building Relationships mini-workshop. He had extensive experience and training in leadership development and had conducted effective trainings for the Department of Health Services in California as well as the Centers for Disease Control.

I would be the opening speaker at the event giving a short welcome address. I was also the closing speaker, providing my evaluation showcase of program success on day two. My presentation focused on the significant findings from a cost-benefit analysis study I'd done with a highly regarded economist colleague from UC Berkeley.

"I also have some good news," I added. "Our USDA bureau chief executive will be available to give a motivational session about building relationships with local state agencies," I said.

"Let's include a staff celebration," I suggested to the group. "We can provide teaching awards to staff members who have been with the program from one to fourteen years," I explained.

"Ginny's prepared a list of those who may be currently eligible," I said. Ginny sent her document via email to the committee members.

"Wow!" Claudia was the first to open the document. "I see there are at least eighty-one staff members who have worked with the program for a year or more," she stated.

"There are about twenty staff members who have been with us more than eight years!"

Ginny volunteered to send the list to each of the program leaders for them to update and correct information. A couple of committee members volunteered to prepare the personalized staff certificates.

"We can do a brief ceremony at lunch," I suggested. "I'll ask the USDA executive if he could hand out each award."

Claudia asked for ideas on our conference title and theme.

Ryan, our IT guy, had made a fancy "hold the date" announcement with a bold picture of California and the San Francisco Golden Gate Bridge!

"How about 'Building Bridges'?" Jonnie suggested.

"Yes!" Claudia agreed. "It works well with our keynote speaker." We all agreed that "Building Bridges" would be a good way to rebuild the community.

The conference call was very productive. We scheduled our next meeting for the following week.

Before concluding the meeting, Claudia announced, "I have a suggestion. Let's all go out to dinner together at the end of the first day." I was pleased when everyone agreed.

"I'll make a reservation at Max's," Ginny, our conference administrator, suggested. She knew it was one of my favorite places to eat.

"It's a very lively and fun restaurant," I added. It would be great to socialize again with my colleagues.

We decided to meet at Max's Restaurant in Burlingame at 5:30 on the evening of the first day. I could already taste the dessert I planned to order their famous hot fudge sundae where the fudge is so luscious that it flows off the sundae and onto the plate below!

⚬⚬⚬

On Monday, November 19, the Internal Audit Report was released to the press. The university included my statement in their cover letter disclosure of public information:

> TO RECIPIENTS OF THE REPORTS:
>
> Portions of three UC Davis Internal Audit Services (IAS) reports dated July 2007 ... have been redacted ... Also it is important to note why references to the whistleblower in these reports were not redacted ... the whistleblower has explicitly indicated a preference for being identified in the report ...

It had been a long and worrisome day. I knew that the media would be reporting the story the next day, the day before our Thanksgiving break, and I worried about more negative attention for the department as well as the college. Would Percy and Lorenzo blame me?

The *Sacramento Bee*'s front-page story was written by Carrie Peyton Dahlberg:

Misuse found in UCD funds

A federal program aimed at teaching the poorest Californians … was misused by the UCD [Food, Health, and Society] department, paying for computers, remodeling and unrelated research, campus auditors said in a report released Monday.

Three heavily censored audits … released by the university in response to a *Sacramento Bee* public request, found that … $2.3 million … dwarfs the original $160,000 estimate made in March when a former … employee was indicted …

The article spelled out the fraud and misappropriation in dollars and cents. Of the $2.3 million, a large amount was attributed to the department chair: $80,522 in salaries and benefits for researchers who worked for Raymond, $11,497 for room renovations, and $101,291 for fancy equipment for the department. Beverly's theft was estimated to be $200,000.

… Instead, using the title of former departmental chairman, the audit states that his "failure to act on allegations of fraud" allowed abuses by one employee to continue …

Other articles were published, and the large-scale negative attention made me concerned about further retaliation. I avoided everyone.

With our conference event approaching, I sent an email to the vice-chancellor requesting approval to present a prepared statement about the audit findings to the conference attendees. I expected colleagues would ask, and I wanted to know how to respond publicly to the hundred and fifty university employees and other professionals who would be attending our conference. I thought it would be better to answer questions openly right at the beginning of the event. I didn't want to stick my head in the sand and hope for the best.

Percy replied on November 29th, the Friday before the event:

> It would be my recommendation that you not discuss any aspect of the audit … more importantly because you are also a party involved in the audit. I believe any statements by you would be taken to be self-serving and, even, to have legal implications …

I found his latter statement cryptic and a bit creepy. Percy went on to say that *he'd* be speaking about the audit findings at my conference.

Percy sent an email to my executive assistant that he'd be attending the first day only. He asked her to book a meeting room so he could meet with everyone. I assumed that this was when he planned to discuss the audit findings, so I arranged a large conference room for him.

I then found out that he'd scheduled his session, "Office Hours with the Dean," from 5:00 to 6:00 p.m.

I reserved the room as instructed and didn't give it a second thought until I heard from a frantic Claudia. She said there was an event planned for Monday after the conference and the committee would have to bow out of our dinner plans. She indirectly mentioned the dean's discussion, but her message was also cryptic.

I suggested we rearrange the dinner for 6:30 p.m. She hesitated.

"Maybe you and your staff should go to Max's without us," Claudia suggested.

"You mean after Percy's event?" I asked, confused.

"Well," Claudia started, "I'm not sure how to tell you this, but I don't think it would be a good idea for you to attend the discussion. It will be facilitated by one of the faculty in your department."

Claudia hinted that it might be better for me to go to Max's and relax, suggesting that others might be less constrained if I wasn't in the room.

I asked Claudia directly about Percy's meeting. She seemed not to know. After a lot of hemming and hawing, Claudia admitted that I wasn't invited. I began to think that she was worried that I might just show up.

How can Percy bar me from attending a meeting at my own conference? I wondered. *Would he have asked me to leave the room if I had walked in with everyone else?* I believed this was another attempt to silence me. I believed Percy wanted to blame me for the fraud and it would be much easier to do this if I wasn't in the room.

I decided not to rock the boat. I thought if I went, or even protested, it would reflect poorly on me for not following orders. I wouldn't have any difficulty finding out what was said at the meeting. All I needed to do was to wait outside the room until one of my more talkative colleagues saw me. I certainly could count on one or more folks who would be happy to pass on bad news!

December 2007

On Monday, December 3, 2007 our two-day "Building Bridges" conference began. I was pleased with the large turnout and, by the end of the day, relieved that no one asked me about the investigation.

When 5:00 rolled around, I sat on a couch about twenty feet from the entrance to Percy's not-so-secret meeting. As I watched everyone walk into the meeting room, not one person acknowledged me. I counted the number of people whom I'd supported with letters of recommendation—at least ten of them were attending the meeting. I sat calmly on that couch for more than three hours.

At around 8:00, when the discussion finally ended, Sierra, a colleague I'd known for decades, was the first to walk out of the room. She saw me sitting on the couch and ran over. Sitting down close to me, she began whispering in my ear: "Do you think the dean supports you?"

I wasn't sure how to respond. *Should I say, Yes he supported me before I blew the whistle?* I answered her question with a question. I had my notepad in my lap and my pen was posed to take extensive notes.

"Percy and I have worked together on this program for years," I answered cheerfully. "Do *you* think he supports me?" I asked, waiting for the bad news to hit the fan! I believed that the dean's office barred me from the meeting with the purpose of letting me take the blame for the negative publicity. I expected that Percy wanted to steer the criticism and scrutiny away from himself and the college.

A small group of people had gathered. They'd just left the room and were watching us from close by. I figured they were wondering if they should intervene. Sierra was someone you could count on to share the good, the bad, and the ugly!

Then it all came pouring out. Sierra said that Percy had convened a meeting to discuss my mental state. She said that many reported that I was clinically depressed and had some sort of mental illness. She told me all about the gossip and who said what during the meeting. She kept patting me on the shoulder and rubbing my back. She repeatedly said that it was important for me to know. I got an earful!

"I really want to help you get through this," she whispered, her face crinkling with angst.

"There are treatments for depression," she advised while twisting and turning on the couch.

"I'm not depressed," I answered simply. The crowd nearby was pacing. Many of them looked worried as they watch Sierra share their secrets.

"The dean was encouraging everyone to share their … ahh … issues about you," she said moving even closer to me on the couch.

"Did anyone try to stop the discussion?" I asked, now mortified that a public discussion was held about Percy's opinion of my mental health. This wasn't something I expected—even from Percy!

"Well," Sierra started to answer my question, "a couple of county directors expressed disdain," she told me, frowning. "Dirk facilitated the discussion," she added this fact to the scuttlebutt. Dirk and I had recently published a paper together.

"Did Dirk say anything in my defense?" I asked surprised that he'd participate in something like this.

"No," she answered. "He appeared to go along with Percy."

When Sierra indicated that Percy believed my illness was too severe for me to continue as director, a new picture emerged. She mentioned several names of colleagues who agreed. This wasn't big news; these were the same folks who'd signed the removal petition, or what I now called the "Percy Commission."

"He said that you should not be directing a multi-million-dollar program," Sierra confessed breathlessly. "He asked for ideas on what to do with the program once you're gone."

"Gone?" I blurted out a little loudly. Then I saw Claudia standing with the audience, looking flustered.

"We spent a lot of time discussing the future of the program. I think that the university will be relocating you, probably down south," Sierra said absentmindedly.

"There was some talk of your getting fired," she continued in a more hushed tone. "I want you to know that it can take several years, probably five, to complete all of the termination paperwork," she added, obviously well-versed in the subject. "My advice," she said putting her hand on my shoulder "would be to retire. How old are you?"

"I'm fifty-four." I wanted to stand up from the couch and announce, *I'm not leaving.*

"Are you taking any medications?"

"No," I said shaking my head. "Sierra, I'm not ill," I said simply. "Did Percy suggest I was on medication?" I asked trying to get critical details.

Instead of answering, she put her arms around me and we embraced. "We've known each other a long time. I'm telling you because I thought you'd want to know the truth," she concluded.

I could see the mob pacing. I figured they wanted to stop Sierra from spilling the beans. I moved closer and whispered in her ear.

"Yes," I agreed. "I do want the truth," I admitted. Clearly, Sierra believed the gossip and rumors were correct; she wasn't even listening to me. I was dumbfounded that this group of academics could be so easily swayed!

"Sierra," I said quietly, "I know you mean well, but I'm not ill—and I'm certainly not backing down. I'm staying and you can quote me on that."

Sierra looked at her watch. A couple of her associates approached to swoop in and take her away. I pictured more gossip in the pipeline.

"Your time is up!" I quipped as she quickly gathered up her purse and notebook, got up from the couch, and trotted off with her colleagues.

Now that the hot seat on the couch was vacant, Claudia ran over to fill it.

"Are you OK?" she asked, looking concerned. Claudia was someone I trusted.

"Did Percy really discuss my mental state?"

"Sierra wasn't supposed to tell you!" confirmed Claudia. "Everyone in the room made a promise to keep what was said confidential," she added, frowning.

"I'm glad she did," I answered. "Did Percy suggest that I was 'too sick to be the director'?" I asked, looking directly at Claudia.

She nodded yes.

"She shouldn't have told you," Claudia said shaking her head in disbelief. I suspected that Claudia wanted to undo the damage that she wrongly believed that Sierra had created.

When I saw Dirk Roman emerge and shut the door, I tried to catch his eye. I didn't believe for one minute that he thought I was ill.

"Did Dirk facilitate the discussion?" I asked Claudia.

She nodded. I'd worked closely with Dirk for years and funded much of his research on poverty. I wondered why he agreed to facilitate this talk-of-the-town meeting. Did he think it was legit because Percy was a high-level dean? I wondered about his role: *Et tu, Brute!*

"Did Percy say anything about my future?" I asked a weary Claudia, who was holding her head in her hands.

"Well," she began uncomfortably, "he indicated that what was going to happen to you was confidential," she replied.

I assumed that Percy wanted his public discussion to be leaked back to me. Did he think that the humiliation would be too much to bear and I'd run away in shame? Or did he expect it would make me angry enough to resign in protest?

These colleagues, former friends, high-level officials, and future leaders were just going to sit back and let Percy trample all over my university career. What would it take to get these folks to speak up?

Considering that question, I suddenly became convinced that what their actions— and most particularly their failure to act—had achieved was ... *nothing!* These academicians would *never* have blown the whistle on wrongdoing. I was strangely intrigued by that momentary insight.

As I collected myself, I asked Claudia one final question: "Did anyone step forward to support my work?" I asked, needing to know where I stood in the academic mob.

She looked down and didn't reply.

"The purpose of this conference—*my conference*—was to build bridges," I said to Claudia, who was now looking at me. I didn't tell her that I felt the mob was trying to burn the bridges down.

"And that's what I plan to do tomorrow," I concluded as I got up from the couch, so much wiser. "I'm taking a stand tomorrow," I told Claudia, "and I'm hoping the group will acknowledge that I'm completely fit for the future ahead of us."

Claudia moved uncomfortably on the couch. She may have wanted to offer some sort of support, but I imagined she believed it was too personally dangerous to do so.

I returned to my hotel room to write up my notes about what I'd heard from Sierra and Claudia. I wasn't sure what the outcome would be—I was still optimistic that I could turn things around. But, in case that wasn't possible, I wanted to be sure that I had a detailed report ready to submit to Investigator Cruz.

Then I focused on how to face the mob with dignity and honor. I wasn't about to roll over and play dead. Percy's displays of power and intimidation only fueled my desire to rise above the fray. This day wasn't going to be my last hurrah!

——◆——

The next morning, I woke up early and went downstairs to network with as many people as I could find. I wanted to show anyone who'd attended Percy's meeting that I was completely fit for the future.

I gave several enthusiastic pep talks during the second day, looking for each of the persons who'd attended Percy's discussion to show them that I wasn't afraid of the dean's office attempts to silence me.

At 1:30 p.m., I stood at the podium ready to give the final presentation at my conference. I'd ordered the hotel's renowned caesar salad for the participants to feast on while I presented my vision for the future. I would focus on my accomplishments—the most recent one: getting $13 million in funding to continue the program and salaries and benefits for most the people sitting before me!

"Colleagues, friends, and supporters, I'm here to thank you for your significant work," I began my voice rising proud and steady. Glancing around the room at those in attendance, I was moved by the feelings that tugged inside me.

I flashed on Mark Antony's ironic speech from *Julius Caesar*: "I come to bury Caesar, not to praise him." Answering the charges against Caesar at his funeral, Antony also aimed to convince the conspirators to break free of the power mongers. I wasn't about to give up and bury my head in the sand!

"Thank you for your dedicated years in assisting California's most vulnerable and culturally diverse families, individuals, and children to improve their life in ways well beyond our nutritional message."

"I want to share with you a number of our program successes in empowering our participants to build a better life for themselves." My voice sang out with warmth. I made sure to include *our* in almost every sentence.

The conference folder included a copy of another accomplishment, a recent publication on the cost-effectiveness research that I'd conducted with a brilliant economist. During my forty-minute requiem, I explained how these results were used nationally to leverage future funding for California.

"It's been gratifying working with all of you over the years to fight poverty. I've been blessed with being able to say, with documentation, that we've made a difference in the lives of millions of low-income individuals, children, and families throughout California. At the end of the day, that's what matters," I trumpeted, hoping that my message rang loud and clear.

My speech closed to hearty applause. I asked the conference planning committee to come up to the podium to thank them for their work on the conference.

After recognizing the committee, I signaled for the finale to begin. The committee walked among the attendees and handed out to everyone my holiday gift: a specially made baseball cap in university colors. The navy blue cap had a message of empowerment in gold. I'd wanted to print *We Are the Champions,* but stuck with the tried and true: our UC logo.

An inspirational song played while everyone put on their cap and cheered. Claudia began a chain dance and we all clasped hands, circling in celebration.

It was a magical moment for me, and a great equalizer. At that final moment, I wasn't the whistleblower who exposed criminal activity—I was just another of those who joined hands in the circle dance, someone who envisioned a society free of poverty.

Arriving at home around five o'clock, I reviewed my draft report on Percy's attempt to smear my credibility. I decided that this was retaliation at its worst. I emailed my report to Investigator Cruz at 5:20 p.m. on Wednesday, December 5th.

"This is clearly retaliation," I wrote. "I'd like to add it officially to my complaint." To me the retaliatory aspects of Percy's meeting would just be the icing on *my* cake!

I expected to hear back that the investigation was completed. I didn't think the university would want to spend money to interview the academic mob who witnessed the public discussion of "my mental state according to Percy Grossman." It would be a costly endeavor for Investigator Cruz to travel up and down the state asking a bunch of county-level nutritionists about their "expert" opinions on the mental health of a colleague.

I felt confident that Percy's final assault on my reputation would be his last. My office temp had completed typing up the evaluation comments from the Building Bridges Conference and sent them to me. I was gratified that the staff had made positive and encouraging comments about the event. I also received high marks for my dedicated leadership to the program. There was no mention of Percy's after-hours mental-illness exposé!

A week after my post-conference email, Ms. Cruz responded that her investigative report was almost finished. She recommended that I contact the Provost's office about the discussion and any future alleged retaliatory events.

The next morning I sent an email to Franklin Taylor-Starr, the LDO, to document Percy's inappropriate public discussion about his views on my mental health. I was confident that this could be considered a serious breach of privacy.

Clearly, the dean's office went out on a limb when they sanctioned this kind of discussion at a university-funded event.

Later that afternoon, I began to feel quite fatigued and went outside my office to get some fresh air. My heart was racing, and after twenty minutes, when it didn't let up, I went inside to consult with my doctor. He recommended I get it checked out.

I was about to take myself over to the nearby Medical Center but decided that it would be safer to ask one of my staff to drive. It was almost 4:00 p.m. I called Ginny Buckner, who came into my office and then ran back next door to get her purse.

Ginny returned to tell me that I didn't look good and she called 911. I wasn't feeling much of anything at this point. I sent an email to Frank, "Ginny called 911," as I heard the ambulance coming. I turned off my computer and started to gather up my work when a large group of firemen, paramedics, and police entered my office with a stretcher.

It was a surreal experience. One paramedic popped an aspirin under my tongue and another reported that my heart was racing over a hundred and fifty beats per minute. I was impressed with how many people could fit in my office! I arrived at the ER about thirty minutes later.

The staff at Sutter Hospital in Davis were very efficient. After many hours' worth of tests, I was told that I'd had an acute episode of heart palpitations and high blood pressure. I was released from the emergency room with instructions to follow up with my doctor in Berkeley.

As if a line had been drawn in the sand, I knew there was no turning back. I'd accomplished everything that I wanted to do: After I discovered the wrongdoing, I reported the fraud.

I cooperated fully with the investigators. I worked with the USDA to get the program back on track. I received another year's funding and brought everyone together to celebrate our new program.

But now it was time to go. I believed that those in power wanted the program directed by a middle-level manager. I didn't want to be the dean's office's puppet, pushing papers around a desk.

My goal was to make a difference in the lives of the most vulnerable. I came to grips with the fact that it was time to return to my academic roots. Daniel Ellsberg had advised me to embrace a new future. It was time to move forward, to return to my former position as a faculty member devoted to publishing and teaching students. I believed that someone with top-notch administrative skills, not academic leanings, should now be managing this critical food stamp education program.

On Tuesday, December 18th, I was officially notified that the retaliation investigation findings were completed. The vice-chancellor told me that much of my retaliation complaint had been substantiated. On that same day I negotiated a settlement with the university to return to my faculty position, a new office far from the fraud, a startup package, and security of employment.

I was also told that I should lay low and stay away from the Davis campus for a while. I was approved to immediately begin a "no-fault" administrative leave, which meant that the time off wouldn't count against my retirement or university service credits.

In mid-January I heard from the Provost's office that they wanted me to read the retaliation investigative report as soon as possible. I assumed part of the whistleblower policy allowed me to see the findings of the report before it was transmitted to the chancellor for a final decision.

But in fact, the Provost's office had a different and much more compelling reason for me to read the report.

6 A Revealing Report

January 2008

It was raining on January 29 when I arrived at Davis. The sole purpose of my journey was to read the retaliation report. I went up to the Chancellor's office and was met by my escort, Tamika Reeves, the executive assistant to Chief Academic Resource Executive Valerie Yu. It was 2:00 p.m.

I was asked to leave my purse in Tamika's office. We got into the elevator and she pushed the button for B2, a basement floor under the Chancellor's administrative building. This floor contained unoccupied offices. We walked down a narrow, dimly lit hallway and found the room assigned to me. Tamika entered the number code on the door lock and opened the door. I could hear the steady stream of rain pouring on the pavement above.

I entered the tiny, cold room. A rectangular metal table and three chairs looked as if they had been sterilized under the long fluorescent light that hung above. I pulled out one of the chairs and sat down facing the door.

I wasn't allowed to bring anything with me—no paper, no pens, no cell phone. Tamika switched on the light and placed a sealed white envelope on the steel table. The fluorescent tubes hummed as the room slowly brightened.

"I'll be back in an hour to see how you're doing," Tamika told me. "Do you need anything?" she asked softly after placing a small packet of Kleenex on the table.

Continuous rain pounded on a narrow window high above my head. Tamika turned, opened the door and I waved goodbye. She nodded back a friendly smile and then locked me into the university's dungeon. I heard the door close, the lock click, and then her footsteps echoing down the empty hallway.

I hoped this report would help me understand why my colleagues were still avoiding me. I had originally thought there would be a rash of wrath and fury from the department where the fraud took place, but now I wasn't sure what to expect. The case was mostly over, so why were folks still in a tizzy? I recalled people being annoyed about the strict program rules and government forms. Were people angry because of the paperwork? Or was there something else?

Still stubbornly fixated on fond memories of my work at Davis, I was hoping to restore trust in the scientific community—especially my former friends, colleagues, and associates. If I could move on, why couldn't they?

Consumed with the need to understand retaliation, I also wanted closure. I recalled the seriousness of the faces when I was told that the report was ready. Both Chief Executive Yu and Vice-Chancellor Taylor-Starr turned white when they said that I'd be allowed to read the report.

Franklin Taylor-Starr told me, "The report is about seventy pages. We have determined that you have a need to know what is in this report; however, you will only be able to read the report over a specified timeframe and some of the names will be redacted."

The window above me shook with the sudden downpour of heavy rain and thunder. As I tore open the envelope, a dream from an erratic night's sleep popped into my head:

I'm lying on a grassy hill listening to Joni Mitch-
ell on my headphones. It's a warm, sunny day
and I feel the rays of sunshine on my face. I watch
a small fluff of cloud drifting slowly across the
bright blue sky. Joni sings, "I've looked at clouds
from both sides now, from up and down and still
somehow ..." More soft pillows of cloudy wisps
float by as she sings, "But now they only block the
sun ..." Suddenly, the peaceful puffs gather into
a large seething mass of gray. The sky darkens,
heavy rain begins to fall. An angry bolt of light-
ning pierces the calm, forcing me to stand up and
run for shelter.

Determined, I pulled out the report and unclipped it. The report's white front cover, dated December 20, 2007, was sterile, bland, ho-hum. Focusing on the title,— "Investigation Report: Administrative Fact-Finding Complaint of Retaliation," I saw the names of Isabelle Cruz and Troy Archer typed neatly underneath. I wondered if this would just be another university report that would captivate my attention for about one microsecond.

The table of contents was devoid of information. Two white pages contained nineteen thick black lines of redaction, probably names of the interviewees. My name stuck out like a sore thumb: *Amy Block Joy, Dr. Block Joy, Dr. Amy Block Joy.*

I relaxed the moment I skimmed the three-page introduction about the purpose and process of the investigation. The background information was concise. I'd read so much about the case that none of this raised an eyebrow. The analytical writing allowed me to distance myself and view the content as a scientist.

I flipped through the report quickly. It was divided into three main sections: interviews, credibility determination, and at the end of the report, the reviewer's conclusions, or "Findings of Fact."

I'd planned to read the report from cover to cover, but I realized I would need to read fairly quickly since I only had the afternoon with it. Armed with three questions, I wanted concrete answers.

My first question concerned Vicki. What did she tell the Dean's office? How did Vicki explain the email that she sent admitting her transgression?

Retaliation was my second and most salient question. How was it orchestrated and who participated? I needed to understand why folks shunned me!

The third was personal: Would the results provide constructive ideas on how to return to my university career?

The first interviewees were folks from the Dean's office. On page 4, I read what Vicki told Investigator Cruz. My first question was answered right off the bat!

Vicki's Accusation

> ... on Tuesday, July 24 ... [Vicki] met with [two unidentified persons from the Dean's office] ... told them about a meeting [she] had with Dr. Block Joy where her tone and persona changed. [Vicki] said Dr. Block Joy showed significant agitation and at one point [Vicki] thought Dr. Block Joy might strike [her].

By the time I got to page 8, it was all starting to make sense—in a soap-opera kind of way. On July 20th, just before Vicki came bursting into my office, she'd met for two and a half hours with Glenda Quinn, the author of the now-famous organizational review report. Glenda had given Vicki another report and discussed it with her—one that I'd never heard of! Investigator Cruz called it a "supplementary report."

This was the moment when I discovered that Glenda had prepared a secret report about me. Vicki, with Glenda's report in hand, then blasted over to see me. She told Investigator Cruz she was "on fire."

I flashed on Vicki mocking me with that tobacco-colored envelope. So, *Glenda's been working behind the scenes all along*, I mused.

I then read Vicki's testimony:

> On the Friday … July 20, 2007, [Vicki] stuck [her] head into Dr. Block Joy's office to talk to her … This meeting was not scheduled … [Vicki] had the report in [her] hand … and started telling Dr. Block Joy … Dr. Block Joy was on her feet screaming … [Vicki] said [she] thought Dr. Block Joy was going to hit [her] and that Dr. Block Joy was "enraged" … "beside herself" … [Vicki] said [she] was pretty rattled by this "Jekyll and Hyde" response and it struck [her] as an abrupt change and abnormal. If [Vicki] had to put a label on it, it would be "manic-depressive."

My heart started racing as I reread what Vicki reported as her testimony. Investigator Cruz added a note of explanation at the bottom of the page:

> [Vicki's] use of the terms "Jekyll and Hyde" and "manic depressive" cause the [Investigators] to suspect that someone in the Dean's office shared their perspectives about Dr.

Block Joy when [Vicki] met with them to
discuss [her] interaction with Dr. Block Joy.

As will be shown ... both [Vicki] and [cam-
pus department] personnel have used these
phrases.

The idea was that Vicki, the dean's office, and the Department of Food, Health, and Society personnel were spreading rumors that I was manic-depressive, and using the same
exact language, as if they'd rehearsed it! I didn't anticipate
seeing this in black and white!

I shivered. It was as though a winter wind were swirling
into the room as the rain pelted on the window behind me.

Recalling Percy's questions about medications and therapy and his mental illness discussion at my conference, I began to see the big picture. Percy was determined to destroy
my credibility by using the tried-and-true method of isolating someone: spreading false rumors about mental illness!

I didn't expect this kind of tactic from a high-level dean
at the university. In fact, I didn't think for one minute that he,
Vicki, or others at the university believed that I was manic-depressive or would use a language like that without prompting.

Vicki's interview continued. Investigator Cruz reported
that Vicki "did not want to work with someone that volatile."

On Monday [July 23, 2007], [Vicki] talked
to Dr. Block Joy, again in an impromptu fash-
ion, and told her that [her] last day in the office would be that Wednesday ... Dr. Block
Joy appeared astounded that [Vicki] was
leaving...

This was a total fabrication. Vicki hadn't told me she was
leaving on July 23rd—or ever. I found out from a staff member while I was out at a site visit.

I recalled Vicki's stoicism during that Monday meeting when I calmly discussed her improper advice to Rebecca. She left my office around 1:35 p.m. She must have read the email I sent her at 1:42. Did she become unglued when she saw that I'd copied the Dean's office?

Investigator Cruz pointed out that Vicki sent an email to the Dean's office two minutes later, at 1:44 pm: "I told Amy that my last day working here will be Wednesday afternoon. I don't think I can work with her productively ... I will tell you more at our meeting [scheduled for July 24, 2007]."

Putting all the information together wasn't difficult. Clearly, Vicki was upset when I called her on the carpet for her improper advice to Rebecca. Her solution was to get out of Dodge!

Vicki's Advice to Rebecca

As I started to process Vicki's fall from grace, I wondered why she'd given such bad advice in the first place. Why on earth would she take the risk of telling Rebecca to use overtime hours to increase her salary? Did the dean's office know of Vicki's blunder? Did Vicki eventually come clean with the investigator?

Investigator Cruz wrote:

> [Vicki] told the group that Dr. Block Joy had accused [her] of telling [Rebecca] to go ahead and submit overtime that [she] had not actually worked ... said that [she] did not recall saying this ... told them at some point that [she] wanted to send an email to [Rebecca] to clarify the policy. [Vicki] did not tell the group that [she] had already sent an email ...

Clearly, Vicki was fully aware that what she'd done was wrong and was desperately trying to cover it up. Vicki then told Investigator Cruz that she thought Rebecca had been routinely using overtime to increase her salary!

> [Vicki] said [she] believed that [Rebecca] had been charging extra hours ... [Vicki] said [she] told [Rebecca] to "keep doing what [she] had been doing." ... Dean's office was upset that [Rebecca] was claiming overtime.

At this point, I'd lost all confidence in Vicki coming clean. I didn't believe that Vicki thought Rebecca was charging extra hours or using overtime inappropriately. Still, I couldn't understand why Vicki would continue down this path.

Vicki's Correction Email

I was very curious how Vicki would explain her email correction to Rebecca. Would she simply deny she sent it? Or would she try to cover it up?

Not surprisingly, Vicki told someone in the dean's office, most likely Shirley, that I bullied her into writing it!

> ... [Vicki] told her that Dr. Block Joy instructed [Vicki] to apologize for giving incorrect information ... [Vicki] told [redacted name], "I'm not going to do that because I didn't give incorrect information."

Vicki's inability to admit that she'd messed up didn't bode well for her. I was reminded of Beverly's inability to face her inner demons!

Vicki's Final Interview

Vicki concluded her interview with Investigator Cruz a few pages later:

> [Vicki] said [she] was initially unwilling to participate in the investigation because [she] did not understand why [her] comments were being taken so seriously and made into a "big deal."

Suddenly, recalling Raymond, my former supervisor, telling me that embezzlement was "no big deal," I pictured Vicki tumbling down the same slippery slope. Investigator Cruz wrote:

> When [Vicki] initially raised that [she] was leaving and the reasons for it, [Shirley] brought in [others from the dean's office] to the conversation. Then [more people from the dean's office were] called into a meeting in the Dean's office attended by [four others] ... "I felt like I was being used to attack Dr. Block Joy" ...

"Yes, Vicki, you were used!" I ranted loudly in the university dungeon, my voice bouncing off the walls. *"Why didn't you speak out and put a stop to it?"*

I heard a soft knock on the door. Tamika had returned; she said I was looking pale. That first hour buzzed by quickly!

Tamika insisted that I should have something to drink and returned with a bottle of water. She lingered for a few minutes in the chilly room and we chatted about our kids. I think I must have looked a bit better after that because she said my normally rosy cheeks had returned.

I told Tamika that I'd only read ten pages! She said she'd come back at 3:30 to see how I was doing.

Vicki's Credibility and the Resulting Findings of Fact

Disappointed by all the Vicki revelations, I skipped to the end of the report to read what Investigator Cruz wrote about Vicki's credibility. The entire paragraph was redacted! I then read Investigator Cruz's findings of fact:

> On Wednesday, July 18, 2007, [Vicki], Dr. Block Joy and [Rebecca] went to lunch together. During the lunch, [Vicki] said to [Rebecca] something like: "[Roland] would probably kill me if [he] heard me say this, but ... figure out what an Analyst would make and record overtime to hit that amount ..." On Monday, July 23, 2007, Dr. Block Joy met with [Vicki] and raised her concern that [Vicki's] advice to [Rebecca] was contrary to University policy. Dr. Block Joy asked [Vicki] to clarify and correct [her] advice to [Rebecca]. [Vicki] wrote an email to [Rebecca] acknowledging that [she] had given [her] improper advice contrary to University policy ... wrote this email on [her own] volition ...

Because the dean's office suggested that I bullied Vicki into writing the email correction, Investigator Cruz added this statement:

> "I find ... assertion to the dean's office that [Vicki] was bullied into writing this e-mail to not be credible ..."

Investigator Cruz then continued:

> ... [Vicki] was embarrassed that [she] gave this advice [to Rebecca] ... was further embarrassed when Dr. Block Joy copied an email to the Dean's office which documented the advice [she] had given.

In the end, Vicki's cover was essentially blown when she tried to explain away her email correction to Rebecca. Investigator Cruz wrote:

> [Vicki] did not raise the issue of [her] alleged advice until specifically asked by me. [She] then indicated that [she] believed that [Rebecca] had been claiming overtime that [she] had not worked, and that [she] had merely told [her] to "keep doing what [she] had been doing" as if this would mitigate the improper advice [she] had given ... [Vicki] ... essentially admits to advising ... to report ... time contrary to University policy.

Investigator Cruz's interviews with Vicki, Roland, Shirley, Percy, Lorenzo, Glenda, Rebecca, and myself were summarized:

> [Vicki] led officials in the Dean's office to believe that [she] had not told [Rebecca] to claim overtime that had not been worked.
>
> ... met with [Glenda] on Friday, July 20, 2007, at approximately 1:00 p.m. ... until approximately 3:30 p.m. ... Around 4:20 p.m., [Vicki] ... knocked on Dr. Block Joy's door to discuss ... holding a copy ... asked Dr.

> Block Joy if they could discuss … Dr. Block Joy told [Vicki] she was busy … The meeting was brief …

Investigator Cruz concluded:

> While I find it difficult to reconcile the two different descriptions regarding Dr. Block Joy's demeanor during this short encounter, I find that Dr. Block Joy did not yell or scream …

I was relieved that Investigator Cruz was able to tease out the facts. All the hours of interviews, reading emails, and piecing together the evidence from other documents that she'd uncovered provided sufficient factual information to determine what had and what hadn't taken place.

Feeling satisfied, I felt that Investigator Cruz had put the whole Vicki brouhaha to rest.

<hr />

The rain had stopped pelting on the window behind me and the light in the room seemed a tad brighter. I felt a rush of adrenaline when I returned to reading the interview section of the report. Glenda Quinn's name glared back at me.

Glenda Quinn

I'd already been able to put some of the Glenda-puzzle pieces together. Vicki met with Glenda on July 20th for two and half hours just before barging into my office wagging a dean's office envelope at me. I hadn't known that Glenda prepared a

confidential report in April 2007. Investigator Cruz referred
to it nonchalantly on page 2 of the report:

> In April 2007, the Dean's office commis-
> sioned an [organizational review (OR)] ...
> among other findings ... recommended
> the program be given additional staff assis-
> tance ... [Glenda] also prepared a Confiden-
> tial Supplement to the [OR] which provided
> additional observations. (Exhibit 4)

I turned to the last page of the report to look for Exhibit 4.
There were no exhibits included in my copy. I wasn't surprised. I was, however, more than curious about what Glenda
told Investigator Cruz about it:

> ...said that [she] produced a second confi-
> dential piece ... because [she] knew that the
> original [OR] document might be dissemi-
> nated to ... Dr. Block Joy ... [Glenda] want-
> ed that piece to be shared freely but there
> were other things that needed to be said that
> should not be in a document that might go to
> Dr. Block Joy ... Dr. Block Joy did not get a
> copy of the confidential addendum.

Wow! So Glenda had created her own version of a James
Bond "For Your Eyes Only" report for the Dean's office. The
use of a bunch of innocent-sounding labels—*supplementary,*
addendum, confidential piece—only exacerbated my feeling
that this was something much more sinister. Did the dean's
office share Glenda's secret report with the USDA?

I continued to search for clues about Glenda's mysterious
Exhibit 4:

> [Glenda] met with [Vicki] on July 20, 2007
> at 1:00 for about two and a half hours ...
> [Vicki was] a bit agitated ... after their meet-
> ing, [Glenda] provided [Vicki] with a copy of
> the supplemental report ... talked about what
> had to be done ...

I then recalled Glenda's confidential notes, or "observations
of Amy" that I'd found in September. Was this just more of
the same?

> [Glenda] ... said the program right now is
> not functional ... is sending notes to the
> Dean's office of [her] impressions of the pro-
> gram which include [her] impressions of Dr.
> Block Joy. Dr. Block Joy is not aware of that
> fact ...

So Glenda didn't know that I found her notes! Investigator
Cruz added a note at the bottom of the page:

> Dr. Block Joy is aware that feedback about her
> is being sent to the Dean's office by [Glenda].
> Dr. Block Joy found a note dated September
> 12, 2007, which contains criticisms about
> her ...

I finally discovered that Investigator Cruz had asked Glenda
about her Amy-notes:

> [Investigator Cruz] asked if [she, Glenda]
> felt it was okay that Dr. Block Joy was not
> aware that feedback about her was being pro-
> vided to the Dean's office. [Glenda] said [she]
> ... does [feel okay] because [Glenda] wants

> to reach a win-win. [Glenda] explained that
> [she] does not have a purview over correc-
> tive or disciplinary action against Dr. Block
> Joy ... is merely trying to evaluate, assess and
> take action to provide the Dean's office with
> information about what she is doing ...

Glenda was asked if she felt bad about doing this behind my back: "... no, I don't feel bad about it ..."

Baloney! I silently growled. This was just another example of an "ends justify the means" rationalization. If Glenda's purpose was to improve the program, then I, as the director of the program should have been given a copy of her "confidential addendum."

At the end of Glenda's interview, I read the following statement: "[Glenda] said she has had no conversations with [redacted person from Dean's office] regarding Dr. Block Joy."

Investigator Cruz wrote: "Again, this contradicts [redacted person from Dean's office's] testimony."

Despite her assertion about not feeling bad, Glenda must have been aware that her contradictions, secret reports, secret meetings, and secret notes transmitted to the dean's office about me weren't kosher!

I couldn't imagine how a middle-level staff employee could write a report that I, as a member of the faculty and the director and principal investigator of a multimillion dollar program, wouldn't have access to.

This is when the real retaliation issue snapped in to focus: What happened to due process? Suddenly I became aware that the very people whose job it was to protect me from retaliation actually looked like they were orchestrating it!

Tamika returned around 3:30. She said that I looked better.

"Yes," I said. "I do feel better." I was amused by Glenda's lack of professional backbone. *Glenda*, I chuckled to myself, *this is no place for amateurs!*

I told Tamika that I wasn't done. Tamika said she'd check back around 4:30. I was ready to read the last section of the report. This section would reveal the retaliation.

Interviews with Amy Block Joy

I was impressed with the factual accuracy and completeness of the accounts of my two interviews (September 10 and October 2, 2007). Investigator Cruz had included them almost verbatim. I turned to the section on credibility and read Investigator Cruz's summary:

> I found Dr. Block Joy to be incredibly accurate about details. She takes extensive notes, keeps extensive files, and has an almost photographic memory of dates and times. On objective facts, she is very accurate and credible.
>
> ... In answer to some requests for information, she provided much more information than necessary in response to a particular request ... sending me over one hundred email messages, many with attachments ...

I returned to the interview section. When I got to page 16, the title "After the Whistleblower Complaint," marked the beginning of the retaliation investigation:

> Since the indictment [of Beverly Benford in October 2006], [redacted] says [he/she] has asked for and received more specific answers

to [his/her] questions regarding whether [he/
she] can remove Dr. Block Joy. [Redacted]
said … that [he/she] had talked to [redacted]
in the fall [2006] about issuing a Letter … to
Dr. Block Joy, telling her she needed to shore
up her program and fix some things … [Re-
dacted] had conversations about potentially
removing her and was told that there was not
a record of failings that would justify her removal … [Redacted] also shared that [he/she]
was told to "tread lightly" because Dr. Block
Joy is a whistleblower … "tried to bend over
backwards not to show any signs of wanting
Dr. Block Joy removed." …

I was pretty sure that the redacted interviewee was Dean
Percy Grossman. I wondered which one of his many bosses
told him to "tread lightly." As I continued reading, I had to
stop and catch my breath. This section contained testimony
from my colleagues and university friends. Page 17, then 18,
then 19 and 20, and on and on contained the most horrific
material. Balanced on the edge of a folding chair, I read the
whole tawdry tale with great discomfort. It wasn't just painful, it was academically obscene.

Smear Campaign

I'd been aware of negative rumors circulating in the department right after I blew the whistle. At the time, I was
alarmed by all the unwelcome attempts to keep me from doing my job. I'd had no idea how far it went. A smear campaign began right after I blew the whistle. Pages and pages of
bizarre comments were plastered within every paragraph of
the report. Reading the testimony of my colleagues was like
trying to run through a maze of molasses—slow, tedious, and

sticky. By page 22, the comments made by those I'd spend decades supporting brought me to my knees.

> ... is the first person who spoke ... about Dr. Block Joy's anger and how she can change and transform into an enraged state ... This occurred in the fall after the complaint was filed ... said, "you won't understand it until you experience it." ... then explained that when Dr. Block Joy gets mad you "see her eyes glaze or change. There is a physical transformation ... she becomes a different person and yells and screams"...

> The second person who told [Investigator Cruz] about Dr. Block Joy's behavior was ... the former chair of the department. Professor ... had the same experience with Dr. Block Joy where he "felt as though there was a physical transformation of [Dr. Block Joy], a tensing of her muscles and a change in her eye quality." Professor ... reported seeing some physical transformation of Dr. Block Joy ... a change in her body, she was not her normal self, and ... saying ... about her "acting possessed" ...

Acting possessed? Startled, I pushed away my rising revulsion.

As I began to recall a number of puzzling incidents, my initial shock turned into a smattering of enlightenment. Remembering the August 13th interrogation with Percy, Lorenzo, and Shirley, I wondered if they were pushing to make me angry. Did they want to witness this so-called physical transformation first hand? Is this why Shirley was trying to locate a good seat in the room?

An even more troubling portrait came in the form of key words: *Bipolar, manic-depressive, Jekyll and Hyde, dual personality,* and *mentally ill.* Was the objective was to humiliate me? If so, their ignorance about mental illness was as alarming as their intent to discriminate.

Dumbfounded by the willingness of folks to go along, I recalled the long history of my program and everyone's enthusiastic involvement. Before I blew the whistle, these so-called scientists now purporting that I was ill were happily spending millions of dollars under my leadership.

Creating and spreading rumors about mental illness is an effective strategy for isolating someone. The stigma about mental illness is so threatening that even intelligent, compassionate people avoid anyone labeled mentally ill. I was sickened by the idea that they would use this to hurt me. Did they think that gossip would force me to throw in the towel and head for the hills? If so, they had seriously underestimated my passion for truth!

Just as I thought I'd heard everything, a new face leaped out at me: Beverly!

Beverly

[Redacted] said that "[she] and [Beverly] became close friends a few years ago … I guess I probably shouldn't be talking to Beverly."

Why were some faculty still communicating with Beverly? I was more than surprised that, months after her indictment, Beverly was still in the picture. I thought of all the people who might have a reason to stay in touch with Beverly: Darci came to mind first. Then, of course, Crystal, Bonnie, Cindy, and others in the department. Suddenly the last piece of the puzzle fell into place: Beverly's case was still pending. Beverly, still pleading not guilty to the allegations of embezzlement and fraud, apparently had an expensive attorney. I wondered who was footing the bill for her legal defense.

Vilification

I continued to read and discovered that my former colleagues had created their own mob mentality of self-righteousness. A lack of evidence, scientific data, or facts didn't deter any of them! Convinced now that these academicians were following orders from the powers that be, I became intrigued by all the gory details.

A faculty colleague, one of Raymond's buddies reported:

> [A friend and colleague] ... thought that Block Joy was actually "guilty" ... duplicitous, ran a poor program, and was unstable ...

> [Another colleague who benefited from millions of the program funds] ... beaten up by the whole Audit process. The Auditors have taken up a lot of her time ... and is not comfortable being questioned ... taking a toll on [personnel in the Department of Food, Health, and Society] ...

> [A faculty member reported] ... budgets are too scary ... could not even understand the budgets. Despite this ... had to go through extensive questioning about the budgets that [she] ... does not understand ...

This faculty member was a colleague I'd felt quite close to—someone who had been quite friendly to me when I arrived at Davis with a million-dollar grant. *Was this about the money?* I had to reassess this so-called friendship after I read

Investigator Cruz's note under her interview: "[She had a] palpable dislike of Dr. Block Joy ..."

> Another one of my friends/colleagues told Investigator Cruz: "[Redacted] has refused to interact with or speak with Dr. Block Joy since she filed her 'anonymous' complaint because 'I was so disgusted by that'" ...

> Another longtime friend, whom I'd supported many times with enthusiastic and heartfelt letters of recommendation, told Investigator Cruz:

> We [in the Department of Food, Health, and Society faculty] are dealing with a complex and ill person ... extremely paranoid ... charming ... manipulative ... I am very happy that something will finally be done about Dr. Block Joy.

> ... said that in meetings with Dr. Block Joy she was very passive ... "I won't work with her" ... the situation came to a head when ... was attending a meeting in [DC] in May of 2007. [She] was under stress of participating in the Audit and had been told not to talk about things with other people ... saw on the news the horror in Virginia Tech ... said it dawned on her that this guy, the shooter was getting all the attention. And she thought, 'This is just like Amy Block Joy, she is getting all the attention and we have all been abused by her' ... said that Block Joy has "cut me in ways that leave me trembling."

> [Redacted faculty colleague] ... had one key incident with Dr. Block Joy ... says that Dr. Block Joy came into her office and started yelling at [her] for approximately five minutes—about a report that had not been done ... [Redacted] "sobbed uncontrollably for days" [and] said the incident was like "Dr. Block Joy had taken a crochet needle and pulled out my heart" ...

I was shocked and stunned by the cloak-and-crochet needle vilification. For the first time since I'd blown the whistle, I had to honestly face the fact that this mob weren't going to change their tune.

I also felt a twinge of sadness—I'd invested so much of my career and life in working with these people! And now, there was no future in working with any of them.

———

Tamika returned at 4:30. I told her that I still hadn't reached the report's conclusion. She made a telephone call outside my room and returned to let me know that I would have to finish up by 5:00. She said that Chief Academic Resource Executive Val Yu wanted to speak with me. I nodded. She said she'd return at five o'clock.

After she left the room, I turned the page and found my former supervisor telling tales.

Former Chair, Dr. Fred Stone

Fred Stone had been communicating to me negative rumors and gossip the whole time. I didn't take it seriously. After all, Fred liked to talk and talk is cheap. Because of university policy regarding his role as my former supervisor, his comments weren't redacted:

> Professor [Stone] told the investigators: "... there are a number of indictments against her ... we refer to these discussions as Amy moments ..."

> Professor [Stone] said: "...she behaves by yelling, irrational ... like bipolar." [Investigator Cruz] asked Professor [Stone] if he'd ever seen the yelling or irrational behavior. He said once they had a meeting in his office that started out friendly [this was in September/ October 2006 just after Dr. Block Joy blew the whistle]. The department needed budget information. Dr. Block Joy said she could not provide it to him because she was part of an ongoing investigation ... then walked out of the room ...

> ... Later when asked about the same incident, Professor [Stone] indicated that she slammed the door on her way out ... Professor [Stone] said he has heard of this behavior from others, in fact, "Virtually everyone who has worked with her has seen this behavior ... everyone knows that she behaves bipolar, including students, county officials, faculty and [Vicki and Glenda] who have been subject to her recent behavior ... said that 'several sources' have confirmed this kind of behavior."

Fred's diatribe was expected. Hugely impacted by the exposure of fraud, Fred maintained his loyalty to Raymond and then retired. His unwillingness to stop the fraud and to report it ultimately sealed both his and Raymond's fate.

It was Fred who'd spoken about a cover-up!

> It became clear shortly after Dr. Block Joy filed her complaint that various folks ... were under considerable suspicion. [A faculty member] said that Dr. Block Joy provided information about what was going on ... because it was a departmental cover-up ...

I turned to the back of the report to check out his credibility:

> First, Professor [Stone] exaggerated his alleged interactions with Dr. Block Joy ... said Dr. Block Joy's public persona is one way but behind doors she behaves by "yelling, irrational ... like bipolar." When asked if [he] had ever seen the behavior, he talked about a meeting ... no specifics regarding yelling or "bipolar" behavior. Later in the interview, he indicated the same incident as evidence of ... anger and mental instability ... that Dr. Block Joy had slammed the door on her way out. In order to get more specific about Dr. Block Joy's demeanor during this exchange, we asked him to re-enact it. After re-enacting the conversation between himself and Dr. Block Joy, he stated that she "just left the room" with no mention of slamming a door ...

Investigator Cruz added: "Unverified and/or exaggerated information has been shared liberally within the [Food, Health, and Society] Department and between the Department and the Dean's Office ..."

Next, Professor [Stone]'s perception of Dr. Block Joy is colored by his surprisingly honest resentment towards her for the unforeseen outfall of her whistleblower complaint ... And based on a report in the *Sacramento Bee* reporting information from a police report, Professor [Stone] has labeled Dr. Block Joy as a force from which the entire [Food, Health, and Society] Department needs protection.

One of my so-called friendly colleagues was also resentful for several reasons, one of them being loss of USDA funding:

[Redacted] has a motive to lie or exaggerate about Dr. Block Joy. Like Professor [Stone], [redacted] is upset that [she/he] has had to be involved in the audits ... is very defensive about having to answer budget questions ... Lastly, [redacted] claims that [she/he] has never seen or read the [petition] that calls for the removal of Dr. Block Joy as Director ... Many of the emails we reviewed call this assertion into question ... [redacted] seems very involved with the [authors of the petition] ...

Both Professor [Stone] and [redacted faculty member/friend]'s credibility is impacted by resentment towards Dr. Block Joy over the decreasing availability of [USDA program] funds ... faculty and [others] historically have benefited from ...

Dean Percy Grossman

The four-page interview with Percy was repetitive and written in third person. The esteemed Dean Grossman had been interviewed twice by Investigator Cruz. I was quite surprised by what he told her:

> [Percy] ... has known Dr. Block Joy professionally for twenty to thirty years ... and that prior to the past year, he never knew of or heard of Dr. Block Joy being short-tempered, yelling, or intimidating people. He had no examples prior to this year of Dr. Block Joy shouting or screaming ...

> ... prepared a summary of complaints made about Dr. Block Joy ... sent to [redacted] on March 1, 2007 ... states that from 2002 to 2006 [he] believed ... program was "proceeding well" ... then states ... "learned differently when [Dr. Block Joy] initiated a whistleblower allegation" ... that Dr. Block Joy had "screamed at, berated and terrorized students and colleagues ...that people were fearful of her and that she seemed to demonstrate a dual personality."

Percy also said that he "had encouraged Dr. Block Joy on a number of occasions to get counseling help."

I was impressed that Investigator Cruz got Dean Grossman to admit that he wanted me out.

> [Percy] believed that she was a director who could be removed ... Since the indictment, he has asked for and received more specific answers to questions regarding whether he can

> remove Dr. Block Joy ... was told [by higher
> levels of the administration] that there was
> no record of failings that would justify her
> removal ... spoke with county advisors who
> were "unloading" about Dr. Block Joy ...
> none of these conversations [were] about her
> shouting, yelling ... intimidation ...
>
> ... said of Dr. Block Joy, "Now she had total
> protection and this is outrageous" ...
>
> [Percy] explained his strategy: "Dean's Office
> is in a difficult position. [The Dean's office]
> can either put in a structure to 'do it,' or they
> can let her take leadership and fail ..."

I assumed "it" meant firing me. He was probably advised that
he wouldn't succeed, so instead, he went down the "let's get
her to resign" path by creating gossip and spreading rumors
to disturb and humiliate me.

Moving around uncomfortably in my chair, I wondered
why Percy would take such a risk? Then I turned the page
and—surprise, surprise—*my husband* entered the picture!

Percy reported to Investigator Cruz:

> The day the letter [from the county colleagues
> requesting that Percy remove Amy Block Joy
> from her director position] came out, Dr. Block
> Joy found out about it and asked for a copy ...
> [Percy] took it to her home in Berkeley ...

Percy was trying to pull a fast one! He gave himself away
when he wrongly stated to an investigator that I lived in
Berkeley. I lived in Kensington. Percy hadn't taken the letter
to my Kensington home—he faxed it to me.

> [Percy] thought her house seemed very disor-
> ganized and ... exhibited that ... she was not
> all well ... said there are major problems in
> Dr. Block Joy's home ...

Huh? Then I read Percy's final sentence and bolted upright in my chair! Percy told Investigator Cruz that he had "heard that her husband is no longer living with her."

Stunned, I read the sentence again. My husband had moved to Berkeley long before I'd blown the whistle, and I speculated this was the "Berkeley home" that Percy visited. However, his going to what he *thought* was my home crossed a line. Percy must have sought out my husband, Leonard, in the hope of getting dirt on me. Staring at the sentence, I had to radically alter my thinking. Leonard was one of Percy's old friends. Had he thought to involve my husband in his retaliatory scheme?

Pressed for time, I continued to read Percy's interview. He spoke about the August 13th meeting when the dean's office confronted me with Vicki's false allegations:

> ... Dr. Block Joy was deflecting discussion
> from herself and [Percy] did not believe her.
> [Percy] thought at that point that she should
> not be working for UC Davis because she is
> "treacherous"...

Treacherous! Was Percy concerned that I was *dangerously* close to figuring out what was going on? More curious than ever, I peeked at the end of the report to see what Investigator Cruz reported about Dean Percy Grossman:

> One example of [Percy's] prejudicial assess-
> ment of Dr. Block Joy was [his] dramatic re-
> sponse to her statements in the meeting of

August 13, 2007 ... "treacherous" and needed
to be fired from University service ...

The Dean's Office

Interviews from folks at the dean's office were interwoven
and scattered throughout the report. I couldn't figure out
who said what. In the end, Lorenzo, Roland, and whoev-
er was responsible for overseeing these deans all distanced
themselves from the gossip and rumors, and in doing so, left
Percy alone on the ledge:

> [Redacted name] ... has labeled Dr. Block
> Joy as a force from which the entire depart-
> ment needs protection ... others in the de-
> partment are aware that Dr. Block Joy was
> the whistleblower and openly talk about their
> annoyance with the audits that resulted from
> Dr. Block Joy's complaint.
>
> At some point recently, [dean's office redacted
> name] was looking for emails that described
> the behavior ... found emails from [various
> persons] wherein [they] made reference to Dr.
> Block Joy having a "Jekyll and Hyde" behav-
> ior. But [redacted] said when ... re-reviewed
> the emails, [he/she] did not see any specific
> reference to shouting or any similar behavior.

By this point, it was clear that Percy was looking high and
low for a reason to get rid of me. I wondered who'd asked
him to do this. I turned back to reread a note that Investigator Cruz had written during her first interview with Percy:

> It is unclear exactly who [Dean Grossman] is
> reporting to and who asked [him] to report
> information about Dr. Block Joy's perfor-
> mance deficiencies to the Dean's office. [Re-
> dacted name] states that [he/she] has had no
> conversation with [Dean Grossman] regard-
> ing Dr. Block Joy.

I did wonder, as Investigator Cruz noted, who'd given Percy
the green light. After all, everyone at the university has a
boss, and Percy might even have two.

Retaliation Findings

My reading marathon was about to conclude. I heard the
clock ticking away my last few minutes as I read the Findings section. Clearly, Percy was the ringleader:

> [Percy] ... has been the main conduit of in-
> formation to the Dean's office and the high-
> er University administration regarding Dr.
> Block Joy's alleged angry and intimidating
> behavior. [He] has relayed stories about Dr.
> Block Joy without appropriate investigation
> and without applying analytical rigor to filter
> out what [he] believes and does not believe,
> and, therefore, what [he] passes on to others.
> [He] has interacted with Dr. Block Joy for
> many years, and says [he] has never person-
> ally seen her anger or intimidation, and had
> never heard anything about these behaviors
> until this year, notably after Dr. Block Joy
> filed her whistleblower complaint.

... prepared summary for [redacted names] contains comments made by others against Dr. Block Joy. However, [Percy] was unable to tell the investigators who made what comments and in what context ... After closer examination in this investigation, many of the complaints ... have not borne out the stories regarding Dr. Block Joy's transformations to out of control rage.

... prepared a summary of complaints made about Dr. Block Joy and her leadership, which [he] sent to [someone else] on March 1, 2007. In the summary, [Percy] states that from 2002 to 2006 [he] believes that the program was "proceeding well." [Percy] then states that [he] "learned differently when Dr. Block Joy initiated a whistleblower allegation ..."

... admits that [lists of persons] may not be credible because of their relationship with [redacted name], who has been impacted by Dr. Block Joy's whistleblower complaint, yet [he] continues to relay their stories as facts.

... is also impacted by [his] shocking honesty about [his] dissatisfaction that the University would take steps to protect Dr. Block Joy as a whistleblower. In meeting with the Vice Provost's office regarding Dr. Block Joy's alleged outburst, [he] became "very worried" that they were protecting a whistleblower. After the whistleblower complaint was filed, [he] took efforts to determine if Dr. Block Joy could be removed from her position ...

Percy even worked with one of my colleagues to try to take the program:

> Lastly, [one of my faculty colleagues and former friend] claims that [she] has never seen or read the letter authored by the [petition signers] that calls for the removal of Dr. Block Joy as the Director ... Many of the emails we reviewed call this assertion into question. [Colleague] seems very involved with the [petitioners]. In one conversation with [Percy] in April 2007, [she] spoke with [him] about whether the campus should become involved in a growing effort from [twenty-five others] to create a second, competitive program ... that would seek to take the program away from Amy ...

Still perplexed about why I posed such a threat to Percy when the case was pretty much over, I read the report's final statement:

> Lastly, [Percy] has a motive to deflect responsibility for the failure ... to Dr. Block Joy ... it is in [his] best interest ...

Exhausted, I reread that statement many times. Clearly, Percy had a lot to lose. As the highest level person in charge of the program and the dean assigned to oversee my department, he'd not done his job.

It would be easy for him to blame me for his lack of oversight— especially if I wasn't around to defend myself.

Retaliation Substantiated

The end of the report, the finding of retaliation, was unmistakable:

> [Dean Percy Grossman] ... failed to adequately investigate this and other claims against Dr. Block Joy regarding alleged yelling, outbursts, and abnormal change to her personality.
>
> Even though [Percy] repeatedly told [redacted names] and others that [he] had not seen this behavior on Dr. Block Joy's part, [he] began repeating this information about Dr. Block Joy to others in the Dean's office.
>
> [Percy] talked to [Food, Health, and Society] Department faculty about various allegations against Dr. Block Joy, including allegations that she has angry outbursts, is bipolar, and exhibits an intimidating change in personality.
>
> When Dr. Block Joy was called in to discuss [Vicki's] allegations against her, [Lorenzo, Percy, and Shirley] were already viewing her with suspicion. In fact ... admits that the group was anxious to see if Dr. Block Joy would exhibit the strange behavior that had been described to them.
>
> [Dean Percy Grossman] ... failed to adequately investigate claims against Dr. Block Joy, lacked care and precision in repeating things [he] heard about her, and has had an odd focus on Dr. Block Joy's personality quirks ... In this way, [Percy] has failed to

take steps to protect Dr. Block Joy's reputation or give her a fair opportunity to respond to issues raised about her.

The conclusion of the investigation was on page 54:

We find there is a nexus between [Dean Percy Grossman's] action or inaction and Dr. Block Joy's whistleblower complaint. The record is clear that none of these rumors about Dr. Block Joy were raised until after Dr. Block Joy filed the whistleblower complaint ... Accordingly, Dr. Block Joy's complaint was a contributing factor to the dissemination of negative information about her, and the resulting damage to her reputation.

I was impressed that the report included the following statement by Investigator Cruz:

Both Professor [Stone's] and [redacted faculty member's] credibility is impacted by resentment towards Dr. Block Joy over the decreasing availability of [USDA program] funds ... faculty and [others] historically have benefited from ... funds ... In fact, Professor [Stone] said that Dr. Block Joy's insistence on following the [USDA] funding requirements ... [was] simply for her to "protect her own backside."

Clearly, the resentment of the fraud case was more than just folks being questioned by auditors and investigators. They weren't getting any more of the USDA funding!

Sadly, none of these former colleagues continued their work to help low-income California families, despite the fact the program continued to be funded by the USDA. Their personal decision to drop out *after* the university put a stop to the fraud was highly suspect.

A note was included at the bottom of the page:

> [Percy] ... stated that the Dean's office could respond ... in one of two ways. It could provide a structure to help the program succeed or it could "let Ms. Block Joy take leadership and fail." While [Percy] did not explicitly state that [he] or the Dean's office had chosen the second route, the record evidences this choice. Eight months after the [OR] was issued and over a year after [Beverly Benford, budget manager] left ... this critical position remains vacant ... Dr. Stone said that ... "faculty have to depend on the accountants and other sophisticated professional[s] to get the work done and to get it done correctly." Yet, nobody seems to acknowledge this same fact for Dr. Block Joy ... Perhaps Dr. Block Joy should be given a chance to succeed with a reliable [budget manager].

I was exonerated just as the clock struck 5:00 p.m. The humming light above me appeared to be sputtering out. Exhilarated and no longer shackled to the retaliatory secrets now revealed, I was ready to go.

In my head, I summarized what the report painfully revealed:

> *My whistleblower retaliation complaint was substantiated.*

Vicki's allegation of workplace violence was not substantiated.

Dean Percy Grossman was the retaliatory ringleader.

Percy dispensed unfair and unsubstantiated gossip and rumors about me.

The purpose was to keep me quiet and make me leave.

Individuals went along with this powerful dean.

Motive: To distract attention away from the failings of the Dean's office?

Percy's smear campaign damaged my reputation and future career.

Lorenzo failed to investigate claims against me, but the report didn't address his culpability. Because there was no retaliatory finding in the report, I could only assume that he'd been cleared.

Having focused so much of my energy on reconnecting with my former clan, I finally awakened in the dungeon at Davis! I wasn't going to allow these soul-crushing tactics to uproot the things that mattered to me.

I heard a soft knock on the door.

"Come in," I said as I put the report back into the envelope. Tamika opened the door.

As we strolled back to the elevator, Tamika was silent. Our footsteps echoed down the empty corridor. As Tamika pressed the elevator button to go the top floor, I gathered up my courage. It was my turn to speak.

I arrived in Chief Executive Val Yu's office at 5:10. I must have looked pretty ragged because she asked me if I felt well enough to drive home.

"I'm OK," I answered truthfully.

There was a long pause as I pulled out a chair and sat down at the table across from her. Two high-level university compliance officers that I'd worked with, Edward Diaz and Felicia Lee, were in the room with the Dr. Yu. I assumed they'd all read the report.

"For the record," I stated, "I'm not bipolar. I'm not manic-depressive. I'm actually quite shocked to have worked so long with these individuals, to have supported them through thick and thin and now to find out that they, well ... that they really don't know me."

I wanted to make a statement about the discriminatory comments made by the UC Davis faculty, deans, and human resources professionals. Mental illness, like other medical conditions, is diagnosable and treatable. I was alarmed by the prejudicial ignorance and misperceptions that were maliciously spread under the guise of academic candor. I wanted to express my outrage right then and there, but bit my tongue. This investigation wasn't over. It would be better to make my feelings known at its conclusion.

"I'm troubled that these individuals thought it was OK to pass on malicious and untrue rumors about me," I stated. "Apparently, this was done to discredit my reputation and personally hurt me."

The university has more work to do, I thought to myself. Championing the rights of those affected by medical conditions, especially mental disorders, which tend to be most stigmatized by society, should be clearly stated in their beloved "Principles of Community." The workforce—at minimum these particular folks, needed to be educated on the basic tenets of privacy, civility, common courtesy, and respect.

I flashed on Percy, feeling that I needed to make some sort statement about his conduct involving gossip, rumors, false accusations. How could a high-level official representing the college do this?

"I had no idea that Dean Percy Grossman was creating a campaign to discredit me and my reputation, and that so many *people* were involved." I wanted to call them *co-conspirators* and to announce that their smear campaign didn't work.

"It was cruel!" one of the compliance officers commented. The remark seemed to bounce around the room, and I could only nod in agreement, lowering my head to fight back tears.

"I'd expected that this fraud case had finished and to see a Case Closed stamped at the end of the report," I admitted. "I had no idea … that this case still continues to plague me."

"I'm grateful that the university retained Investigator Cruz," I said pointedly. "She and her faculty reviewer did a thorough investigation."

I looked around the room before making my final statement.

"I cannot continue to work with any of them!" I announced. I finally realized why I was allowed to read the report before the chancellor had made a decision.

"Thank you for providing the administrative leave," I concluded. It dawned on me that university policy couldn't provide guidance on what this report so painfully revealed.

I shook everyone's hand before saying good-bye and left the room quietly. Alone, I took the elevator and exited through the empty atrium on the first floor. The air outside was fragrant from the late afternoon showers. I left the university building and heard the heavy door lock behind me.

One door had closed but now was the time to open another. I was more determined than before. Reading about the campaign to keep me silent had given me more courage. I found my voice: I was ready to stand up and speak out.

Under a moonlit sky, I walked confidently back to my car. As I buckled my seat belt for the long drive home, I wondered what would happen to the university's Investigative Report on Retaliation. This six-month investigation wasn't cheap. I started adding up the hours of interviews as well as my hundred plus emails and attachments over the four-month timeframe: *$100,000, or more?*

The good news for me was that my complaint of whistleblower retaliation was substantiated. I expected that the chancellor would take the appropriate steps to ensure that this didn't happen again to me or anyone else.

As I thought about the findings, I realized that this written report was now subject to public disclosure. After all, it was the citizens of California who footed the bill. I expected that the college would be required to train the workforce on policies prohibiting retaliation.

I fantasized how they might accomplish this. Would they distribute a memo via email with the university's policy against retaliation? Maybe they'd create a new poster and distribute it to all the Davis departments of the College of Innovations. I pictured a bright red poster exclaiming *COI is a Zero Retaliation Zone!*

Perhaps the investigative findings would be incorporated into the Office of the President's Whistleblower Policy. Since that 2002 mandated statewide UC policy is so outdated, this could be a positive first step.

Or maybe there'd be a cautionary statement posted on the university's newly established Whistleblower Hotline: *Warning— The University does not tolerate abuse of power!*

7 | Settlement

"Welcome everyone, and thanks for coming!" I announced standing on the podium at the University of California Davis campus bookstore.

Inspired by the size of the audience seated in front of me, I looked around to see if I recognized anyone.

"My name is Amy Block Joy and I'm here today to share my story—my cautionary story—about my whistleblower experience at the University of California."

It was Thursday, April 14, 2011, and I was speaking about my newly published memoir, *Whistleblower*. I took another quick glance and spotted a friendly face in the front row. Albert Stein, a famous physicist and a good friend was chatting with a character from the book!

"The purpose of my book is to educate future whistleblowers and universities," I read from the author's note in my book.

Three years had passed since my visit to the university dungeon, and I felt strangely serene returning to the scene of the crime.

"I want to begin by thanking all the auditors and investigators for their work on this case, including the Internal Audit team at UC Davis, the UC Davis Police, the university investigators, and other officials from the Office of the Provost," I acknowledged enthusiastically.

"I am grateful that the university launched a full investigation on my whistleblower case," I said holding my head high to make sure everyone could hear what I was about to tell them.

"I wrote most of my book during the administrative leave that the university had arranged after the fraud investigation was completed," I said slowly as some latecomers joined the crowd.

Whistleblower focused only on the fraud case and I'd carefully avoided any mention in it of the retaliation investigation. Having waited over three years for some sort of tangible response, I was concerned that Investigator Cruz's report had been shelved. I'd hoped Davis would make changes in their procedures—or at the very least—openly communicate their retaliation protection policy. Sadly, nothing at this campus had changed.

But I had changed: I'd found my voice. The system wasn't working and someone had to sound the alarm! I wanted to create a roadmap to stop retaliation, workplace bullying, and collegial discord by speaking out about things that mattered.

"It's hard to believe it's been five years since I blew the whistle here at Davis in 2006." I held up my book to show off the image of a "diamond-studded" whistle on the cover. It reflected my personal triumph. My daughter had given me the cubic zirconium whistle the year before for Mother's Day.

"I'm going to tell you about some real events that happened here in 2006," I started. "Although, I have used the real names of many of the people in this story, I have also fictionalized others," I added not providing any clue about which ones were fictionalized.

Facing the crowd of mostly academics, campus staff, and students, I opened with a short introduction about my thirty-two year career at the University of California, beginning with my undergraduate and graduate work at UC Berkeley, my initial academic employment at UC Berkeley and the Office of the President in Oakland, and my last two decades at UC Davis working as a scientist and educator to help the most vulnerable low-income families in the state.

"I'm a big fan of the University of California, and my primary goal after blowing the whistle was to keep my job. I cherished my work in fighting poverty," I said smiling to my friend in the front row.

More people had arrived and the comfortable sofa-like chairs facing me were now filled with friendly faces. I noted others standing among the bookshelves pretending to read a book. Were they worried about attending due to the reappearance of publicity about the case?

In fact, to my delight, an article by Pat Bailey had been published in the UC Davis faculty and staff newsletter, *UC Dateline,* just after my book was released:

Whistleblower writes memoir about UC Davis case

In August 2006, UC Davis … Amy Block Joy officially became a whistleblower, alerting campus officials to what she believed were fraudulent activities … Written partially in the "roman a clef" novel style, in which the identities of many real people and the specifics of actual events are disguised, Block Joy's book also describes snubbing and other inappropriate reactions on the part of some of her colleagues … UC Davis investigated those issues … Block Joy did experience retaliation in response to her whistleblowing, and in 2010, [UC Davis] reached a settlement with her of $89,611.

I was certain to be asked about the money and I was prepared to discuss it openly. My settlement agreement contained no secrets. I'd already given a couple of talks in the Bay Area, where I lived, and was well practiced on answering even the most personal questions. For me, the best part was hearing the audience gasp in shock as my story unfolded. I knew, however, this UC Davis audience would want more. I expected this crowd wouldn't beat around the bush. They'd want to know about the settlement I signed on April Fool's Day, a year ago.

I brought a copy of the settlement document and placed it next to a glass of water on the podium shelf. I'd highlighted a couple of the passages that I felt were relevant to my presentation.

In a hushed tone, I began with the discovery of a hand-written note on a financial spreadsheet.

"At the time, I had no idea what it meant," I stated. "But, like the pulling of a single thread from a sweater, everything started to unravel." I illustrated the thought by tugging a little on my own white sweater.

I decided to introduce the fraudster to the audience right away.

"One of the antagonists in this story was a charismatic woman named Beverly Benford. Officially my program budget manager, I considered her a trusted and loyal colleague," I said choking back the chill of betrayal. "Beverly and I worked closely for twelve years."

"The *Davis Enterprise* reporter Cory Golden published an article on January 26, 2011, that I believe will provide insight on Beverly," I said as I picked up the newspaper to read out loud:

Whistleblower paid a price for reporting theft at UCD

Beverly Benford was a dream to work with. It turned out, though, that even as she charmed her UC Davis co-workers and anticipated her boss' every whim, she stole money from a program teaching nutrition to thousands of the state's poor.

"She was a model employee," Amy Block Joy, under whom Benford worked ... said. "I would have never said to myself, 'My goodness, she's very prompt at getting things; she's efficient; she gives me reports; she flatters me; she's by my side; she comes to my defense— oh, she must be embezzling.'

"It was the biggest shock ..."

I put down the article and began telling the tawdry tale, beginning with my suspicions when the note on the spreadsheet led me to discover my office files locked, and then, after getting Beverly to unlock them, finding a questionable purchase order.

"After I saw the purchase order, I immediately thought embezzlement! However, University policy dictated that I report the allegation of misuse to my boss, the department chair of the Food, Health, and Society Department at the University of California, Davis campus," I stated fiercely.

"But a voice in my head signaled fear. Dr. Raymond Savage, department chair and my supervisor, was a well-known, powerful, highly regarded scientist. Because he liked Beverly, I was concerned that a theft allegation might not go over well and that he might want me to forget about it. My integrity wouldn't allow me to do that," I noted letting that message sink in.

"Put yourself in my shoes," I told the audience. "Besides a question of integrity, this issue had multiple consequences. If I don't report it, I could be accused of covering up misuse of federal dollars. If I do report it, I'm essentially accusing a loyal, dedicated, and popular colleague of stealing!

"So, I had to think hard about what would be the right thing to do," I said, describing my dilemma. "I wanted to give Beverly a chance to explain and I also was required to report my suspicions to my supervisor.

"I arranged a meeting with both Beverly and Raymond. Before the meeting I did some research," I explained. "In this case, I combined a full day of soul-searching while watching a few episodes of *Law and Order*," I added. The audience chuckled at the idea of a scientist conducting research on TV.

While anchoring my book in my hands, I read the scene where I had confronted Beverly with allegations of embezzlement written in a letter that I read out loud to her. My supervisor, the powerful chair of my department was in attendance.

> Beverly stared blankly, not showing any emotion, and not looking at either of us.
>
> Raymond kept staring at the letter, stunned and silent. He wasn't moving at all and certainly not looking at me. One hand was on his chair, his fingers still drumming ...
>
> His face was white, and he was uncharacteristically quiet. He lowered his head and he was shaking it in what appeared to be disbelief ...

"After reading out loud my brief letter, I asked Beverly one question," I told the audience.

"I said, 'Beverly, where is the DVD camcorder?' And she answered: 'It's in my garage.'"

My audience was on the edge of their chairs.

"Although I felt relief that the issue was now out in the open, the question was now what to do about it?"

In my next breath, I explained what followed after Beverly confessed to buying the DVD camcorder for herself.

"I argued with the chair about reporting the misuse up the chain of command. Guess what happened?" The silence in the room was deafening.

"Nothing," I told the audience. "Nothing happened. My letter disappeared into the chair's secret vault.

"Undeterred, I decided to pressure my supervisor into action. My strategy," I stated, "was to put the ball squarely in Raymond's court: I wrote an email to him asking his permission to report the misuse up the chain of command—or requesting that he do so himself.

"I expected Raymond to do the right thing," I told the group. "Instead, he told me that this happens all the time at UC Davis. And in fact," I said clearly, "I was told that this was no big deal and I was the one overreacting!"

I glanced at the audience. Their stunned response gave me solace.

"Eventually, Raymond got the message and told me to consult with the vice-chair. The vice-chair initially gave me hope, but in the end he also had me writing more letters for the secret vault. Apparently, no one wanted to report the misuse to the dean's office!

"What led me down the road to become a whistleblower wasn't Beverly's $1400 purchase order. It was moral outrage. I came face to face with the fact that no one was listening."

A hush fell over the room as I looked around and spotted Marshall T. Truthworth, a colleague who'd telephoned me over the weekend. He told me that several flyers announcing my speaking event had been torn down and found in the garbage. The *California Aggie* reported the incident in an article written by Martha Georgis on April 13, 2011:

Book event to showcase instructor's emotional tell-all

Author encourages future whistleblowers: ... "The message you get is that people want you to leave ... whistleblowers tend to leave but I love my job, and I made a decision early on that I would stick to it as long as I could" ... retaliation still continues ... Flyers of Thursday's book event have been torn down in certain departments around campus ...

I put my book down on the podium.

"The moral outrage that I felt led me to report all my allegations, using the Whistleblower Policy of UC Davis," I said. "At that time, the reporting process included two one-page forms. One form was to report the allegation and the second was to request protection as a whistleblower. One could report the allegations anonymously, but I chose to sign my name because I believed that this was my duty and the right thing to do.

"There was no turning back," I said solemnly. "Everything unraveled after I blew the whistle. A day later, someone, and I suspected it was Beverly, filed a whistleblower allegation against me. I was served in my driveway on a Sunday with a number of charges, including misuse of government property. I was warned not talk to anyone, and this increased my isolation from both my colleagues and friends," I sighed.

"A few days later, the case was turned over to the internal auditors on campus, then the police and later federal agents from the Office of the Inspector General," I continued with the urgency to tell all.

"It turns out there was much more to the case than one rogue employee. Beverly was also turning in fraudulent travel expenses, which had been signed by the department chair. There were other expensive items purchased by Beverly for the department over a six-year spending spree. The high-priced equipment, room renovations, and research weren't appropriate expenses under the federal program guidelines. I didn't know about any of these purchases—it was all done behind my back. The total university liability added up to more than two million dollars!"

My audience appeared satisfied with my summary of the story and I quickly decided to finish up my talking points and leave time for discussion. Questions and comments at my earlier events in Berkeley provided a forum that was both educational and personally gratifying.

"You're probably wondering what happened to Beverly," I said. I looked around to see people nodding.

"Well, at the beginning, Beverly was contrite, admitted responsibility, and apologized for her lack of judgment. She wrote a check to the UC Regents for $1400, although lacked the funds in her account to pay back the money," I added, chuckling.

"Although the initial investigation began with $1400 in embezzlement, this was just the tip of the iceberg. In the end, her fraud was $160,000. The federal agents served a warrant on her home at the end of October 2006 and found tons of electronic goods and evidence of her selling items on eBay.

"Beverly was indicted by the grand jury and the U.S. Attorney prosecuted her case beginning in March 2007. She pled not guilty for two years. On June 10, 2008, she was offered some kind of deal. She pled guilty and was sentenced to one year and one day in federal prison."

I read from Denny Walsh's article in the *Sacramento Bee,* reprinted in my book:

Ex-UCD employee pleads guilty to theft

A former University of California, Davis, employee pleaded guilty Tuesday in federal court to theft of government property ... Beverly Benford of Sacramento admitted a six-year spree of spending federal funds on hundreds of items for herself, including iPods, camcorders, digital cameras, home security systems, televisions, stereos ... She admitted misidentifying purchases to make it appear they were appropriate expenditures. In other instances, she lied about where the items had been delivered to conceal her theft ...

I concluded with a passage from the final chapter of my book:

Beverly entered the Federal Correctional Institution for Women on February 17, 2009, to begin her one year plus one day sentence. Using the "Inmate Locater" on the Web, I confirmed her arrival ...

After I put down my book, several hands shot into the air. I pointed to a gentlemen standing in the back of the room.

"And what happened to you?" he asked from the book shelf aisle.

I swallowed and wondered how much to reveal at this point in the discussion.

"You ask a very relevant question," I began. "My goal throughout the whole investigation was to keep my job—and I'm happy to say that I'm still employed by the university," I said smiling.

While speaking so intimately about my employment, I glanced quickly at the promise I'd highlighted in my settlement agreement:

> Each of the parties, on behalf of themselves, agree to waive and release and promise never to assert any and all claims against the other party and that party's [sisters, brothers, family, entities, officers, shareholders, agents … blah, blah, blah …] arising from or related to your employment with the University of California …

I didn't mention the settlement, instead moved on to my other concern.

"Initially, I was also concerned that the fraud allegations might end the program. The USDA appeared to support my continuation as the director. We removed all the fraudulent components from the 2007 budget and prepared a new 2008 budget that was fraud-free. I did receive another $13 million for that 2008 year.

"However," I continued with renewed vigor, "the fraud investigation triggered a number of spin-offs," I began, deciding to skip any mention of the dean's office.

"After getting another year of funding for the program, I stepped down as director so that the newly funded program could continue without further distraction," I said. "A new director was hired and the program continues to thrive."

"What kind of spin-off?" A voice from behind the bookcase bounced around the room. I nodded to the shelves as though they'd spoken.

"A few months after I stepped down, I received a frightening letter from the university notifying me that I was under investigation again—for the third time! The charges included failure to stop fraud, grant mismanagement, incompetence as a principal investigator, and gross negligence. Anyone of those charges could lead to my dismissal."

Many people in the room scowled in disbelief. I continued.

"I spent a couple of months preparing a three hundred–page defense that I believed would clear me and my reputation. In the end I was grateful to have the opportunity to clear my name."

I paused briefly. I didn't want to reveal that these frightening allegations were another attempt to blame me for the fraud. I felt like I was the university's public enemy number one.

"Were you cleared?" Albert, my faculty friend asked calmly.

"I turned in my written defense in September 2008," I said cheerfully, "and was officially cleared in March 2009. It was a wonderfully liberating moment," I added beaming with happiness. "After that investigation was completed, I was provided an office far away from the scene of the crime," I said trying to make light of my plight.

For a brief second, a haunting memory captured my attention: Fifteen minutes after that wonderful quiver of freedom, I was accosted in the hallway, and this incident created a new dilemma. I shoved that distressing memory aside.

"So what are you doing now?" I heard a voice speaking from the audience in front of me. Relieved, I realized I'd been clutching my book as if it provided some sort of calming effect.

"Thanks for asking," I said directly to the person who raised the question. "Things are definitely quieter now that the case is over," I said cautiously. "I'm teaching a new undergraduate class called Eating Green: Trends in Nutritional Ecology, working as an associate editor for the UC *California Agriculture* journal, and have been involved in some national review panels," I said.

A women sitting on a couch chair leaned forward to ask: "What was the university's response to the fraud?"

"That's an important question," I highlighted. "The university made a number of clarifications and changes in their financial procedures. I'm glad that these issues have now been addressed and corrected.

"One important change is that department heads and others involved in making financial decisions are required to sign a new form stating that they will report wrongdoing," I continued.

"It's hard to believe that high-level officials are required to sign a form to do the right thing," I said. "But, in fact, this was one of the biggest lessons that I'd learned from the experience: Doing the right thing doesn't come easily."

Happy to talk about the idea of doing the right thing, I decided that I wanted to acknowledge that the university also did right by me.

"The university also provided security of employment," I began. "I signed a settlement agreement on April Fool's Day, 2010," I said, chuckling at the irony. "In the agreement, I promised never to assert any further claims of wrongdoing regarding this whistleblower case." A hush fell over the audience.

"So my hands are tied!" I waited for someone to ask about the settlement agreement. I glanced down at it, ready to recite the passage out loud.

> You acknowledge and agree that your Retaliation Complaint, and all of your other grievance(s), reports of wrongdoing, and allegations of misconduct have been resolved to your satisfaction, and that you agree to take all actions necessary to dismiss and/or withdraw any outstanding grievance(s), with prejudice,

as soon as possible after this Agreement be-
comes effective.

No one asked about the settlement. I continued, "I do feel
that the case has been resolved satisfactorily," and pointed to
a raised hand.

"Do *you* feel vindicated?"

"Yes," I began, "as a university employee," I said clearly,
"I feel that the investigation was done fair and square and all
the allegations of wrongdoing were satisfactorily resolved," I
repeated with renewed confidence.

"However, as an academic, educator, and scientist, I want
to make sure that this doesn't happen to anyone else. I've
developed some take-home lessons from my personal experience," I added with gusto.

More hands went up.

"What about retaliation?" someone in the third row
asked.

"There were many forms of retaliation that I experienced
over the long haul. The worst was the silence and ensuing
isolation. People just wouldn't talk, communicate, or even
reply to my emails," I answered, pushing away memories of
Vicki, the dean's office's entrapment, Percy's malicious gossip, and all the other attempts to get me to leave.

"I'm pleased that the university thoroughly investigated
all the allegations," I concluded without any reference to Investigator Cruz.

"Did the university have to pay any fines?"

"'The university negotiated with the USDA and returned
$2.3 million dollars'," I, said reading out loud from UC Da-
vis's press release about my book.

I saw a hand frantically waving nearby and pointed to the
questioner.

"Could you say more about the retaliation?" asked a young woman with a soft voice, adding, "If you don't mind talking about it."

"This is a predictable consequence for anyone blowing the whistle," I began. "There's been a range of reprisals from those who were disturbed by the fraud investigation. In the beginning, right after I blew the whistle, someone, and I think it was Beverly, the fraudster, filed a whistleblower complaint against me."

I waited for the information to sink in. This was something I wanted future university officials to plan for. There should be a way for policy to protect the whistleblower from being sidelined.

I told the audience about the petition to remove me from office and then read from my book the advice given to me by the famous whistleblower Daniel Ellsberg:

"'The turning point in this story is when I sought guidance from my neighbor, who happens to be Daniel Ellsberg,'" I began, holding up my book to read the passage aloud.

> Daniel talked about the road ahead. He said, "Few people will understand what you feel … Remember it's you that will sleep better knowing you did the right thing. Accept your new life now and try to embrace it as an opportunity."

The room became brighter as light filtered through the windows. I paused momentarily to reflect on the warmth of the sun.

I looked around the room while listing some of the various incidents I'd reported: the tampering with my mail, illegal entry of my university office, and that my computer was used by the fraudster.

"And a lot of untrue gossip and rumors were spread about me," I stated without going into any details. "Also," I added quickly to sidestep the gossip issue, "my car was vandalized in the university parking lot."

In my previous talks, the car incident was usually the one that created the most gasps. I looked around to find another hand in the air.

"Did you ever feel threatened?" asked a young student sitting next to the window.

"Well," I began nervously "it's a common retaliation experience," I stated. I was trying to block out the flashback that was sending an urgent alarm to my brain.

As I grabbed the water glass before I started coughing, I glanced at the highlighted settlement sentence next to the glass:

> Additionally, you also reported an incident wherein you allege that you were inappropriately pushed and shoved by a University official ...

For the next ten seconds my mind became fixated on that March 2009 incident. As I raised the glass to my lips, the flashback replayed.

—————

I was leaving the UCD provost's office, having just read the letter that officially cleared me of gross negligence. Elated, I went down to the first floor to drop off paperwork at the dean's office before my meeting with the vice-chancellor. In the hallway, a familiar face approached me— that of a high-level official whom I'd worked with over the years.

Smiling, I said a quick hello as I was about to pass by him in the hallway. But walking right up to me, he stopped, blocked me from moving forward, and began a tirade about an email he'd sent.

He barked something accusatory at me like, "You haven't replied to my email!"

"Email?" I was alarmed by his overbearing tone.

"I'm curious, who told you that you had to use your own funds to pay for office supplies?" he snarled. "Who said that?"

I recalled the email notification that I received from the dean's office about an account that had been set up for me. The $30,000 in the account had never been communicated to me.

"Ah ... I will ... look at your email again," I replied, both confused and agitated. I was certainly not going to discuss this in the hallway. The funds had been allocated more than a year before, and I was planning on requesting an extension of time to spend them.

"I'm meeting with the vice-chancellor," I said calmly. "I'll answer your question later today," I promised.

"I want an explanation now," he announced, quite beside himself. I put my briefcase down on the carpet next to my feet.

"I really need to go," I said softly, "I don't want to be late for my meeting with the vice-chancellor." I waited for him to take a step back away from me.

Instead, he moved closer, his nose looming toward mine. As I stepped back, I saw a flash of anger.

I picked up my briefcase. He lunged forward, shoving me with his shoulder. The unexpected push on my left shoulder forced me to step back. Regaining my composure on two feet, I listened for his apology.

He said nothing.

Stunned, I turned around to see him storm off. I expected to hear a *sorry*. Shaken, I left the building and walked swiftly to my car.

In my car, I found his email on my BlackBerry. He had notified me that a $29,725 balance in my account was going to be returned unspent. I'd replied that I didn't know that I had an account and had been buying office supplies using my own funds. I assumed that I'd get reimbursed at some point after I was no longer under the "about to be dismissed" gun. Obviously my response had triggered him!

I phoned someone from the provost's office to discuss the incident in the hallway. Although I was inclined to walk away from another obstacle in the resolution of my retaliation complaint, I was encouraged to report it to the vice-chancellor.

Arriving at 10:00 for my meeting with Vice-Chancellor Taylor-Starr, I reported the incident. Frank and his associate took notes as I provided details on the encounter.

"The person pushed and shoved me in the hallway," I stated. "The person shoved me with a shoulder."

"Shoulder?" Frank asked to clarify how this happened. I drew a picture on my notebook to illustrate the encounter.

"Yes, the person's left shoulder pushed me on my left shoulder," I said pointing to the two stick figures I'd drawn side by side. The official's stick figure was larger than my own because in reality he towered over me.

"And who did this?" Frank asked me.

"I don't feel comfortable telling you," I said. "I'm reporting the incident, but I don't want to reveal the person's identity."

"The university has an obligation to review the incident," he advised. Frank told me that I needed to name the individual for the university to investigate any alleged violence in the workplace.

My mind raced ahead to the possible consequences of revealing this person's identity. Was it likely to happen again?

Did I have a moral obligation to identify the person? Would this be the right thing to do?

"OK," I said. Clearly this was a moment when I had to make a decision that would affect my future at the university. If I refused to identify the person, then I was giving in to the intimidation. In fact, not telling Frank could jeopardize my credibility at a time when I'd just been cleared.

After a long pause, I told Frank.

"It was Bradley Danner, the dean's office's high-level consultant," I told him. "Brad pushed and shoved me in the hallway. It wasn't an accident. He didn't say sorry. I felt frightened."

Frank was stunned and probably wished he'd not pressed me to tell him. But it was too late. The university was now put on notice and obligated to review the incident.

———— ❖ ————

I swallowed the water slowly and managed to return the glass to its proper place on the podium. Looking back at the audience, I shook off the memory of Bradley, Percy, and Lorenzo. The whole saga was over and they'd all moved on. The unspent $29,732 was returned to the university coffers. Instead, I received $25,000 start-up package sufficient for my future plans.

A hand was waving at me with some urgency. When I nodded, she stood up and announced boldly to the audience:

"I'm a character in the book! I'm Joanne Willow and I was the first to challenge Beverly!"

I beamed fondly at her. She was a colleague who'd reached out to me after reading my book, and was one of a few courageous persons who had confronted Beverly. Like me, she had been rebuffed by the bigwigs! We'd happily reconnected and were now friends.

"Thanks!" was all I said, trying not to disclose any information about the unidentified characters in my book. At an earlier event at Davis, I'd been told that a character in my book had walked into the store, announced he was in "that book" positioned next to the register, and then promptly purchased five copies!

———

At 12:55 p.m. I was ready to call it a day. A young man in the back asked me, "Do you have any advice for others who might find themselves in the fray?"

"My advice is plain and simple: decide what's important. For me, my goal was threefold: report the wrongdoing, continue the program, and keep my job." My book wasn't written to encourage anyone to follow in my footsteps. Many would find the rigors of whistleblowing just too frightening.

I moved closer to the microphone. "Read the organizational policies and know the process of reporting wrongdoing," I affirmed. "Pay careful attention to timelines and write down your report. It will be much better to have spelled it out in your own mind before telling anyone else.

"Next—and this is very important—find someone you trust within the organization. I recommend to report first inside the organization. Check that your organization has a protection policy, and make sure that you sign the form that you want to be protected from retaliation."

I paused and then articulated with passion: "And lastly: document, document, document!"

"What about stopping retaliation?"

"Yes," I said loud and clear. "This is an important consideration. Retaliation is common and predictable. Unfortunately, it's difficult to prove that it happened."

Although I had a lot to say, I decided against expressing any personal disappointment. I was sad that UC Davis hadn't enhanced its own protection policy. For three years, I'd been waiting for tangible changes in enforcement, policy, training/education, organizational structure, and, at the very least, administrative communication. But it was as though nothing had happened at UC Davis. Could it be that this university campus protected only the most powerful?

"In my opinion," I said aiming to be short and sweet, "organizations need to raise awareness about retaliation and educate their workforce that it's a form of bullying and an assault to the organization's code of ethics."

"Do you regret the experience?"

I smiled warmly. "No, I have no regrets. Now and then, I recall the loss of my former life and past career. What I discovered was that this personal journey created new friends and a new vision of how I want to live the rest of my life," I sang out.

"I think the lesson that I learned was more personal than theoretical," I mused. Thinking about my new insight into my inner passion to make social contributions, I added, "You can make big changes by simply following your heart," I finished.

I looked at the clock on the wall and said, "One last question."

A woman sitting in the back asked a question that made me grin: "What did you tell your family? Did they support you?"

In a blink of an eye, I suddenly flashed on my daughter and stepped down from the podium holding my book in one hand.

I moved closer to those in the front row. I didn't need a microphone to answer this intimate question.

"I was told repeatedly not to talk about the investigation to anyone, and I didn't," I said, my voice steady. "At the time, in 2006, my daughter was a senior in high school and applying for college. And, as we all know, this is a pretty stressful experience. I didn't want to overwhelm her or me with the realistic fear that I might, as the family breadwinner, lose my job," I added choking on the memory.

"When the fraud story was published in the newspapers," my voice rising, "I was finally able to let her read what happened at Davis and to me. My daughter knew Beverly, so I expected this to be a big shock."

I cradled my book lovingly in both hands. Gazing around the room, my eyes settled on Gracie, my new faculty friend. She silently nodded, indicating our kinship. Besides being someone who questioned authority figures, she was a mother too.

"I'll never forget what my daughter said after she put the paper down on the couch and looked up at me."

I paused, and took a deep breath as my eyes teared up.

"My daughter said—'Mom, I'm proud of you.'"

References

Prologue

Amy Block Joy, *Whistleblower* (Point Richmond, CA: Bay Tree Publishing, 2010).

Chapter 4

Marion Nestle, *Food Politics: How the Food Industry Influences Nutrition and Health* (Berkeley, CA: University of California Press, 2007, page 107).

Chapter 6

Joni Mitchell, "Both Sides, Now" (1967).

Chapter 7

Amy Block Joy, *Whistleblower* (Point Richmond, CA: Bay Tree Publishing, 2010).